A Parent's Guide
to Understanding
and Responding
to Bullying

The **Bully Busters** Approach

Arthur M. Horne

Jennifer L. Stoddard

Christopher D. Bell

Research Press ∘ 2612 North Mattis Avenue ∘ Champaign, Illinois 61822 ∘ (800) 519-2707
www.researchpress.com

Composition by Jeff Helgesen
Cover design by Linda Brown, Positive I.D. Graphic Design, Inc.
Printed by United Graphics, Inc.

ISBN-13: 978-0-87822-596-5
Library of Congress Control Number 2007939536

To the Bully Busters team, past, present, and future, with thanks for the commitment to helping children, families, and educators—and, in the process, the lives of all people—to be better

—AMH

To all those interested in the growth and development of children and families

—JLS

To my coauthors, who've shared their path with me and, in doing so, enriched my life

—CDB

Contents

Figures and Tables

Acknowledgments

A book such as this is never the product of the authors alone. We wish to acknowledge the wonderful contributions made by many to help this project come to fruition.

Families with whom we have worked

We have had the opportunity of working with many families, participating with them to help reduce bullying within their families or to solve problems of bullying directed toward members of their families. They have been encouraging, supportive, and enthusiastic—and have shared openly their concerns, conflicts, and exasperations. They have courageously taken on problems posed by aggression in other children, sometimes neglectful schools, and cultural directions that often work against a healthy childhood. We respect them for their commitment and dedication to their children and to reducing the problems of bullying in their families, communities, and society at large.

Students who have contributed to the project

We have been so fortunate to have had a team of graduate students—going on 15 years now—who have recognized the importance of the problems of aggression that children and adolescents face and who have committed their time, energy, creative thoughts, and leadership skills to help make the process work. They have participated in program development, conducted parenting and teaching groups, facilitated data collection and analyses, and have been supportive in all the ways graduate students are able to be encouraging. Special mention goes to students who actively led groups in the last few years. In addition, previous graduate students who have gone on to productive careers and still work to reduce bullying in their communities include Dawn Newman-Carlson, Christi Bartolomucci, Natasha Howard, Aaron Turpeau, and Jenny van Overbeke-Brooks.

Colleagues and fellow faculty

A large number of our colleagues and fellow faculty members are devoted to reducing bullying. They share freely of their ideas, thoughts, and recommendations, and they have thoroughly enriched our knowledge of the field of bullying reduction. Our colleagues

Pamela Orpinas, Tracy Elder, and Katherine Raczynski, who have worked on our GREAT Schools and Families Program for years, have been prolific contributors to understanding and intervening with aggressive children. Their ongoing support, input, and creativity has led to continual learning and growth in the field. Bill Quinn, a member of the GREAT program team and a developer of his own model of family intervention for reducing aggression in students, the Family Solutions Program, has offered wonderful input and recommendations for our program. Brian Glaser and Georgia Calhoun, who direct the Juvenile Court Counseling and Assessment Team in Athens, Georgia, work with adolescents and their families and serve as regular consultants and advisors to our program. Their contributions have been very beneficial. The faculty of the Department of Counseling and Human Development Services at the University of Georgia provide an environment of support and encouragement and are always available with their creative ideas and recommendations, and we appreciate their ongoing interest in our bullying reduction program.

Bullying prevention specialists

Many specialists in bullying prevention are highly committed, and they are always supportive, cooperative, and encouraging in their work with us. Susan Swearer and Dorothy Espelage have been enormously helpful and have become dear friends (though still excellent critics). Dave Jolliff, Sandy Moliere, Bill Voors, Amy Nitza, and Brian Dobias of the Bully Safe Schools Program (**www.stopbullyingnow.net**) have been working closely with us as we have developed and refined materials, and we prize their creative input. Others who have shared freely of their ideas and thoughts on helping to reduce bullying, sometimes in person but often through their writing and training, include John Hoover, Dennis Maloney, Nicki Crick, Shelley Hymel, Stuart Twemlow, Gilbert Kliman, Sue Limber, Marlene Schneider, Sheri Bauman, Ken Rigby, Richard Hazler, and Daniel Olweus. Jean Baker has been a close colleague and contributor to our programs on reducing aggression in students, focusing particularly on families, and Randy Kamphaus has been a steady contributor through the ACT Early Project, which he, Jean Baker, and I conducted. Roy Martin has been a delight throughout the process of helping with data analyses and general thinking on the problem. Aleta Meyer, Al Farrell, Pat Tolan, David Rabiner, Robin Ikeda, Tom Simon, and LeRoy Reese have been major contributors to understanding the problems of reducing aggression, particularly with family interventions, through our Multi-Site Violence Prevention Program, supported by the Centers for Disease Control and Prevention.

Research Press

Karen Steiner has been "the other author" of this text; she has devoted enormous energy and talent to the development and refinement of the book, and without her guidance and excellent editorial skills, this book would not have come about as it has. Thanks so much for the excellent work and commitment to excellence for the manuscript. Russ Pence, Gail Salyards, and Dennis Wiziecki, and all the Research Press team, have become dear friends and colleagues. Their ongoing support, good humor, and awareness of the trade are invaluable and cherished.

Others

We always know that, in a writing process, major contributors to the development of a product such as this will be unintentionally overlooked. It seems inevitable that persons important in the process of going from a problem to the development, implementation, and distribution of a program for helping young people will not get adequate recognition for their outstanding contributions. Our apologies for this; we know the ideas and interventions come from many areas, many places, and we appreciate the level of commitment and care that people all over the world are expressing for young people experiencing the pain of bullying. It is our sincere desire to stop the problem, and we appreciate all who are taking their stand to contribute to reaching this goal.

Introduction

Imagine getting off of work following a particularly long and busy week. To unwind, you've decided to meet some of your co-workers for a relaxing dinner at a local restaurant. Everyone agrees to meet there after work. You show up a few minutes late, recognizing some of your co-workers' cars in the parking lot while you circle, looking for a parking spot. You can't find a space nearby, so you decide to park down the street. As you get out of your car, a few individuals catch your attention. They start walking toward you. You begin to feel uncomfortable—you sense that they might be dangerous. Your steps quicken, and you avoid eye contact as the group gets closer. As you cross the parking lot, you realize that they are blocking the door of the restaurant. You begin to feel more scared now since you are still too far from the restaurant to call for help. At this point, the group has cut you off from the restaurant, and they are beginning to surround you, taunting you and making threats. Your heart is pounding, your hands are sweaty, and you have begun to feel dizzy. Just at this moment, when things seem like they are about to get bad very fast, a police officer happens on the scene. The officer approaches you and the group surrounding you. You feel relief instantaneously, firm in your belief that this authority figure will resolve the matter for you. Quickly, you begin telling the story of how the aggressors have been taunting and threatening you. The aggressors immediately chime in, denying your accusations by saying that they were simply walking down the street, minding their own business. After hearing both sides of the story, the police officer says, "Well, this seems like something you should be able to resolve yourselves" and walks away, leaving you in the midst of the aggressors to fend for yourself.

This example may seem absurd, but situations like this one actually happen on a regular basis in schools and communities across our nation. Frequently, children and adolescents do not report bullying to parents or teachers and are left to deal with these problems alone. And in too many cases, even when bullying is reported, adults fail to respond effectively. Therefore, helping kids learn to report bullying behaviors safely and effectively to parents and teachers is very important, as is learning to manage bullying problems effectively when they occur.

Bullying: A Widespread Problem

Bullying has been, and continues to be, a major problem for our children. While many of us can certainly remember being targets of bullying in our own youth, bullying looks very different today. Unfortunately, it has become more intense, more aggressive, more highly sexualized, and more potentially damaging to our children's overall self-esteem and well-being.

Bullying has become such a concern that the World Health Organization created a bullying survey to investigate the experiences of more than 15,000 youth in U.S. public schools. Findings reported in the *Journal of the American Medical Association* indicated that 47 percent of boys and 36 percent of girls reported having participated in bullying in the 12 months before the survey, with 11 percent of boys and 6 percent of girls reporting being bullied on a weekly basis. A Centers for Disease Control study found that 35.9 percent of youth in grades 9 through 12 reported being in a physical fight in the preceding 12 months—and 18.5 percent reported carrying a weapon (gun, knife, or club) in the past 30 days. It's not surprising, then, that a significant number of students feel afraid to go to school: The CDC study reported that 6 percent of the students surveyed did not go to school on one or more days during the past 30 days because they felt unsafe at school or on their way to or from school.

We know that bullying varies from school to school, but if your child is in school, you can be certain that he or she has had a bullying experience of one sort or another. In all of the schools in which we have worked, students report bullying to be one of the major problems they face each day. Even though teachers often don't recognize the extent of the problem, the physical, emotional, and educational consequences of bullying are significant both to the children who are the targets of bullying and to those who do the bullying. Our experience in schools indicates that parents, teachers, and other school staff can't manage the problem of bullying alone. They need the involvement and support of families.

Fortunately, as parents, there is a lot we can do to help. Although much of the bullying that our children experience happens at school or in the neighborhood, both common sense and science tell us that some of the most effective solutions start at home, with the family.

While tackling the problem of bullying, the family must remain strong and supportive, and continue to build upon their strengths and positive values. Therefore, this book embraces a strength-based approach to helping parents, an approach intended to help families communicate better and become more emotionally intelligent. The case examples included in this book are based on the experiences of real families, and the many activities described help parents apply the information they learn about bullying to their own families and circumstances.

This Book Is for You

Although many schools have begun active campaigns to reduce bullying inside their own walls, parents are often understandably confused about how to join in these campaigns and how they can best help their children. If you are concerned about bullying in your child's school, this book is for you, whether your child is engaging in bullying behavior or is the target of bullying. This book is also for you if your child is a bystander, indirectly involved but directly affected by witnessing or hearing about bullying and victimization.

The Bully Busters Program

This book attempts to address questions and concerns from parents we have worked with over the last decade while helping schools implement the Bully Busters program. This bullying prevention and intervention program, successfully used in schools across the nation, is described thoroughly in the two *Bully Busters* books referenced at the end of this introduction.

Your child's school may have adopted the Bully Busters program. If that's the case, this book will help you understand the program. Even if your child's school does not offer Bully Busters, this book provides a solid foundation for helping you assist your child in dealing with bullying situations. It promotes understanding of the nature and extent of bullying, as well as of the impact bullying has on children's lives, self-esteem, and overall development. Specific activities are included to help families confront the issue of bullying, support their children, and increase the quality of life for all involved.

Chapter Overview

Because children who bully and their targets are part of an ongoing cycle of behavior—*the bully-target cycle*—one child's behavior can't be completely separated from another's, and we encourage you to read the following chapters in order, even if a chapter doesn't appear to relate directly to your child's role in the problem. To understand bullying, it's necessary to have a clear picture of how children interact in the situation—as well as an understanding of how the school environment can affect the situation for better or worse.

Chapter 1: Increasing Your Awareness of Bullying

This chapter gives a working definition of bullying and talks about some differences between aggressive behavior, bullying, and normal play. It also challenges some persistent myths about bullying.

Chapter 2: What Causes Bullying and What Can We Do?

It isn't possible to say for sure exactly what causes bullying. However, a number of risk and protective factors at the child, family, school, community, and societal levels play a part. This chapter identifies these risk and protective factors, stresses the importance for parents of knowing what is and what isn't in their sphere of influence to change, and identifies a number of resources parents can look to for assistance.

Chapter 3: Tools for Strong Families

A discussion of general guidelines for healthy and happy families introduces this chapter. The chapter next describes tools that parents who participate in our Bully Busters program have found helpful for keeping their families strong. Equally valuable for children who bully and their targets, these tools include the Family Council meeting, the Big Questions, emotional intelligence and emotional coaching, modeling of positive attitudes and behaviors, and specific strategies for maintaining a positive relationship between parent and child.

Chapter 4: Understanding Children Who Bully

This chapter focuses on children who bully. It describes different types of bullying: aggressive, passive, and relational. It also looks at two special cases of bullying—sexual harassment and cyberbullying—and describes the differences between boys and girls as far as bullying is concerned.

Chapter 5: Understanding Targets of Bullying

Children who are targeted by bullies are also of different types: passive targets, provocative targets, and targets of relational bullying. This chapter looks at their similarities and differences. We pay particular attention to the targets of relational bullying and to bystanders—a group often not recognized as being victimized by the bullying experience.

Chapter 6: Helping Children Who Bully

In this chapter, we take a look at ways to help children who bully. We begin with a list of warning signs for bullying and at-home suggestions for parents to help children who tend to be aggressive. Skills for children who bully are discussed next—these include anger and impulse control, cognitive retraining, empathy, and problem solving.

Chapter 7: Helping Targets of Bullying

This chapter begins with a list of warning signs for targets and suggestions for relating to these children at home. It goes on to describe skills for targets concerning friendships, assertive communication, and asking for help. We consider both ways to help bystanders and ways bystanders can help other children who are targeted by bullies.

Chapter 8: Parents and Schools

This chapter looks at the characteristics of good school-based bullying prevention and intervention programs and makes specific suggestions about ways to communicate and work with the staff at your child's school. It also offers suggestions for empowering parents to work together.

Chapter 9: Taking Care of Yourself

Stress is not necessarily a bad thing—it's an unavoidable part of life that can cause us to grow and change in positive ways. However, too much stress, or distress, can be harmful. This chapter gives general recommendations for coping with stress and describes some specific things you can do to manage stress: become aware of the sources of stress, practice stress reduction strategies, and ask for help when you need it.

About Language

The words and labels people use to describe children and adolescents involved in bullying situations are important because they influence the way we think about these individuals. Rather than label a child a bully, we prefer to say *a child who bullies* as a way of indicating that our purpose is to stop bullying behavior and change the nature of the child's relationships with others, not to put the child into a fixed category, with little hope of change. Similarly, we prefer to refer to a child who is bullied as the *target* of bullying, rather than the victim, because the term *victim* implies weakness and helplessness and also does not express an opportunity for change. Based on our experience with children and adolescents, we believe strongly that bullying can be stopped and that children can be empowered to be more effective in their interpersonal relationships. Whenever possible, we have tried to use the language to reflect those beliefs.

About the Activities

As mentioned previously, this book includes numerous activities for parents and for parents and children together. Some of these are designed to help you acquire basic knowledge about aggression and bullying. Some ask you to take an honest look at your feelings and become more conscious of your family's strengths and weaknesses. Some invite you to think about what you can do to intervene in a bullying situation involving your child or to reduce the problem of bullying for all children. We encourage you to complete as many of these activities as you can—and to discuss your responses with your parenting partner and other parents who share similar concerns, if at all possible. As a group committed to change, we can expect to accomplish far more than we could hope to accomplish as individuals.

References

Centers for Disease Control and Prevention. (2006). Youth risk behavior surveillance—United States, 2005. *Morbidity and Mortality Weekly Report, 55* (No. SS-5).

Horne, A. H., Bartolomucci, C. L., & Newman-Carlson, D. (2003). *Bully Busters: A teacher's manual for helping bullies, victims, and bystanders (Grades K–5).* Champaign, IL: Research Press.

Nansel, T. R., Overpeck, M., Pilla, R. S., Ruan, W. J., Simons-Morton, B., & Scheidt, P. (2001). Bullying behaviors among U.S. Youth: Prevalence and association with psychosocial adjustment. *Journal of the American Medical Association, 285*(16), 2094–2100.

Newman-Carlson, D., Horne, A. M., & Bartolomucci, C. L. (2000). *Bully Busters: A teacher's manual for helping bullies, victims, and bystanders (Grades 6–8).* Champaign, IL: Research Press.

1 Increasing Your Awareness of Bullying

This chapter is about becoming more aware of bullying—identifying what bullying is and encouraging you to explore your thoughts and feelings about the problem. To get started, we give a working definition of bullying and talk about some differences between aggressive behavior, bullying, and normal play. The remainder of this chapter looks at myths about bullying that some parents and teachers continue to believe and that may contribute to the persistence of bullying. We challenge these beliefs—and we invite you to do the same.

A PERSONAL VIEW

In working with parents, we've discovered that they usually remember incidents of bullying from their school days vividly and that they still have very strong emotional reactions about them, whether they were the target, a bystander, or even the bully. It's worthwhile to ground yourself in your own experience before you delve into this book more deeply. You may be surprised by your recollections and responses.

ACTIVITY 1.1

Take a few minutes and think of a bullying incident from your youth:

► Who was involved, and where did the incident take place? What happened in the incident?

_____

_____

_____

_____

► What role did you play in the situation?

_____

► How did you and others in the situation react?

_____

_____

► How did you feel?

_____

_____

► How would you expect your child to react to the same incident?

_____

_____

WHAT IS BULLYING?

When we conduct workshops, we find that the parents we work with often have a general understanding of what bullying is, but they may not have the words to describe it. In this book, when we refer to bullying, we are referring to behavior that is characterized by three qualities, known as the *PIC criteria:*

P—Bullying is *purposeful.*

I—It is *imbalanced.*

C—It is *continual.*

So, bullying is intentionally harmful behavior committed by an individual child or group of children, directed toward an identified child, who is the target. The relationship between the child who bullies and the child who is targeted is imbalanced—that is, the child who bullies is more powerful or of higher status than the target. Finally, the harmful behavior is repeated over time.

Sometimes children are picked on or teased in a single incident. When that happens, it is wrong and can be quite serious, but it isn't bullying, strictly speaking. That's because to be considered bullying, a behavior must be continual, or ongoing.

Consider the bullying incident you described in Activity 1.1:

▶ How does your description match up with the definition we just gave?

_____

_____

▶ Did your description include any of the PIC criteria? If so, which ones?

_____

AGGRESSION, PLAY, OR BULLYING?

We want all forms of aggression and violence in schools, communities, and families to stop. To accomplish this, it helps to be able to determine whether a situation is aggression, play, or bullying. As you read the following, keep in mind the PIC criteria.

Aggression

Although all bullying is aggression, not all aggression is bullying. For it to be bullying, the behavior must happen continually, over time. For instance, someone might occasionally drive aggressively or otherwise behave in an insensitive manner, but those acts don't generally have the impact that the intentional and repeated offenses of bullying have. A single aggressive act might be brushed off as "a jerk doing jerk things," whereas bullying can have a permanent impact on the life of the person at the receiving end. One of the worst outcomes of bullying is that the bully's target develops "anticipatory fear"—an expectation that the bullying will happen again. It is that ongoing fear that is so damaging. Consider the driving example we just gave: Can you imagine how you would feel if the same driver cut you off on the same road every day? You would likely experience anticipatory fear as you approached the intersection. Unfortunately, the same is true for millions of schoolchildren each day—on the bus, in the hall, on the playground, and in the rest room.

Play

Sometimes children engage in rough-and-tumble play or playfully tease one another. A key distinction between this sort of play and bullying lies in the nature of the relationship between the target and the bully, as well as in the intent of the interaction. In play, even rough-and-tumble play, kids enjoy the interaction and share in the winning and losing alike. In bullying, the situation is not enjoyable for the child being bullied, and there is no give and take in the behaviors—only take. Table 1 shows the differences between play and bullying.

Bullying

Following are some examples of behaviors that we've seen in schools. As you read them, apply the PIC model to determine whether the incident is normal play, bullying, or simply aggression.

Raymond

Raymond is new to school and is walking down the crowded hall toward his classroom. As he walks along, he is bumped by a bigger kid who just keeps on going, paying no attention to Raymond.

Clarke

Clarke is also new to school and has only been there a few days. Ever since he arrived, two other boys have teased him about being new and called him names. He is beginning to dread going to school.

Roberta

Roberta has been in school for some time but has not been able to make friends. She has been excluded from groups at lunch and has not been chosen for any teams during recess. She has made attempts to be included but has been ignored. The other girls just walk away from her. She feels more depressed every day.

LeRoy

LeRoy has a new book bag with an authentic athletic team insignia on it. Three other boys tell him to give them the bag. LeRoy says, "I've given you my lunch money, but I'm not giving you my bag. Why don't you guys just leave me alone?" At that, the boys snatch the bag and push LeRoy to the ground, kick him, and then walk away with the bag, leaving LeRoy furious but not knowing what to do.

Table 1   Play versus Bullying

Play	Bullying
► Voluntary	► Coercive, ordering, demanding
► Turn taking	► Doesn't share or take turns
► Equal in size, power, or experience	► Larger, faster, stronger, or having socially imbalanced characteristics
► Give and take; winning and losing possible; shared experience	► Bully always wins
► Enjoys the experience	► Demands the experience

Bill and Ralph

Bill and Ralph get off the bus, walk to a wooded vacant lot, drop their book bags, and go at each other, wrestling each other to the ground. They roll around, tussling, and finally Ralph pins Bill to the ground. They get up, dust themselves off, and go at each other again. This time, Bill gets the best of Ralph. Ralph says, "Okay, let's go best two out of three," and they start again, both laughing.

In the first example, the behavior directed at Raymond reflects an aggressive act, but it is not bullying. In Raymond's case, the bumping was aggressive, but we don't know whether it was purposeful (P)—on purpose or an accident. We know there was an imbalance (I) of power because the other student was bigger than Raymond, but we have no indication that the aggression will continue (C). The incident meets the definition of aggression but not bullying.

Clarke, on the other hand, is a target of bullying. The behavior is purposeful (P), there is an imbalance (I) of power (the other boys have ganged up on Clarke), and the boys have harassed him more than once, making it a continual (C) problem. Thus far, this is an example of verbal bullying, but verbal bullying can escalate to physical bullying, and physical bullying is almost always preceded by verbal interactions such as teasing or name-calling.

Roberta is being bullied because the girls have purposefully (P) excluded her, there is an imbalance (I) of power, and they have been excluding her for some time (C). This is therefore an example of bullying—in this case, relational bullying, in which a group uses their peer influence to exclude and hurt another person.

LeRoy's example is also bullying. The behavior of the other boys is purposeful (P), there is an imbalance (I) of power, and the behavior is continual (C); it happened before, when the group took LeRoy's lunch money. This situation involves physical bullying and is also indicative of delinquency, since the boys stole the book bag.

In the last example, we have no indication that Bill's or Ralph's behavior is either aggression or bullying. The behavior is purposeful (P), but both boys appear to be about equal in power. This is an example of rough-and-tumble play. Though some might confuse this with aggression, it is important to remember that the behavior in this example is performed by children of basically equal status who are participating voluntarily and seem to be having a good time testing themselves against each other.

MYTHS ABOUT BULLYING

As we've said, many people hold beliefs about bullying that just aren't true—the beliefs, in fact, are myths. When we work with parents, we try our best to dispel these myths. Here are several of the most common ones—along with our responses. As you read these myths, think about which ones you may have accepted as true.

Bullying is just "kids being kids."

Although some parents see bullying as a rite of passage for children, behavior that is hurtful to other children is never acceptable and should not be tolerated. Many bullying behaviors have been "normalized" in our current culture—and behaviors considered normal are usually not identified or corrected. Parents may not think that it is their place to get involved, or they may see these behaviors as acceptable because they appear so often in popular media. Just because a person does something a lot, and it is shown on television, does not make it right. A basic principle of bullying prevention is that if it hurts others, it has to stop.

It's not really bullying if no one is physically hurt.

When asked to define bullying, many children provide examples of physical bullying, such as shoving, pushing, or hitting. Rarely have children—or adults for that matter—given us responses such as name-calling, social exclusion, or gossiping. These are also forms of bullying. Bullying takes many forms, and all forms should be stopped. In fact, very few physical bullying incidents ever occur without having been preceded by verbal abuse. Name-calling and teasing can easily escalate into physical fights, and though we've all heard the adage "Sticks and stones may break my bones . . ." we all know that it is not true—words *can* hurt.

Bullying happens only on the playground.

We have learned from our work in schools that bullying takes place in many areas of the school and community, not just on the playground. In fact, the school bus and the cafeteria, as well as rest rooms and playgrounds, seem to be very common places for bullying to occur. Basically, there is an increased potential for bullying in any location where children are not monitored by adults.

Children will outgrow bullying—there are no lasting harmful effects.

Bullying is not a behavior that is specific to a certain age group, and bullying behavior does not stop once kids grow up. On the contrary, if bullying is not addressed early, it is likely to escalate, turning into acts of violence and habitual aggression and even criminal behavior. Many targets of bullying remember their traumatization well into adulthood. These memories can impair the development of one's personal identity and self-esteem, making it difficult to engage in meaningful and trusting relationships throughout life.

Some children are just born rough, and there is nothing we can do about it.

Some children do have more risk factors than others for bullying behavior—for instance, temperament or conditions in the family in which they are raised. Some children are more intense from birth on, whereas others are more easygoing. However, risk factors don't *make* a child become aggressive or engage in bullying behaviors. It is well established that bullying behavior is learned and can be corrected if children are taught more acceptable ways of responding to stressful or difficult social situations and are given the opportunity to do so.

It's best for parents, teachers, and other adults to just stay out of it.

Actually, the opposite is true. Parents and other adults are in the best position to provide safe, effective ways of dealing with bullying situations. With good intentions, many adults tell children to work out their differences, but given the fact that bullying involves an imbalance in power, many children cannot be expected to resolve their problems fairly. Children do need to learn skills to manage conflicts, but there are times children need—and deserve—adult protection and assistance. In fact, when children are left on their own to resolve conflicts, they may resort to extreme measures to stop another child from picking on them. It is much better for an adult to intervene early and teach children effective skills for stopping conflict rather than have to deal with serious injury or damage done by ignoring the torment children receive. Just as nobody tells their child to "go figure out how to tie your shoes yourself," neither should a parent leave a child to figure out conflict resolution on their own. If we spend time teaching our children the simple task of tying shoes, shouldn't we invest much, much more in teaching them important skills to resolve conflict?

Children who are the targets of bullying are bringing it on themselves.

As parents, we sometimes wonder if some children might be doing things (intentionally or not) to bring bullying on themselves. Though it is true that children who are "different" in some way are frequently targeted by bullies, no one deserves to be the target of bullying. Despite the fact that some children provoke negative attention from their peers, this is not true of every target of bullying. Some are singled out even though they do nothing to provoke negative attention. And even those who provoke negative attention from those around them deserve and would greatly benefit from learning the social skills that will enable them to elicit positive attention from others.

Weaker children benefit from bullying. It builds character and gives them an opportunity to "stick up for themselves."

Character education is best done in a nurturing, encouraging, and supportive environment, not in an environment that creates fear and intimidation. People don't tend to learn effective coping skills when they are under threat and stress. Children are no exception to this rule.

If bullying takes place at school, there's not much I can do to help my child change the situation.

It is true that the majority of bullying occurs at school and at school-related functions, such as riding a school bus or attending after-school activities. This does not mean that there is nothing to be done, however. When parents are concerned about the welfare of their child, they can have enormous influence on outcomes at school by working with school staff. Often, a few concerned, involved parents who press for bullying prevention and intervention efforts can get teachers and school administrators to make changes. The efforts of those silent heroes can have untold positive effects on the entire school.

Only boys bully.

When we ask individuals to talk about bullying, many children and parents provide examples that involve boys. But bullying is also very common among girls. In fact, children who bully are "equal opportunity offenders." Research shows that girls bully almost as much as boys, and the already small gap is closing. This myth may arise from the fact that boys are more likely to express their bullying physically, making it out in the open and easily observed. Girls tend to engage more in relational bullying, in the form of rumors, social exclusion, and the like. However, a scary trend is that the gender gap in physical bullying is closing as well.

Girls are targeted for bullying only by other girls.

The assumption that bullying doesn't cross gender lines may arise from the fact that the type of bullying girls most commonly employ is relational bullying. This type of bullying takes place more or less "behind the scenes." Although the majority of girls' bullying is relational and directed toward other girls, girls can and do engage in physical bullying of both girls and boys.

There's not enough time to address the problems of bullying.

Ignoring a problem does not make it go away. In fact, if bullying among children is a problem, without intervention it will likely escalate, becoming more destructive and taking even more time to address in the future. When children are left on their own to resolve conflicts, sometimes targets don't know what to do and may resort to extreme measures to stop another child from picking on them. It is much better for an adult to intervene early and teach children effective skills for stopping conflict rather than to deal with serious injury or damage.

Paying attention to complaints just encourages tattling.

It's important to consider the child's goal in the complaint. Is it revenge, or is it problem resolution? Tattling is an attempt to get someone else in trouble, not a request for help. Having the child come and talk to you about a problem is almost always a positive sign. It indicates trust that you will help resolve the problem. It is important to spend time talking with your child to come to a mutual understanding of the differences between tattling and requesting help. Make certain that your child knows that if he or she needs help, it is available but that you won't support attempts to get other children, including siblings, in trouble.

ACTIVITY 1.3

Think about the myths just described:

► Which ones, if any, did you believe were true?

_____

_____

► Has endorsing any of these myths prevented you from taking action in a bullying situation? In what way?

_____

_____

_____

► How do you think challenging these ideas may change your behavior in the future?

_____

_____

SUMMARY AND CONCLUSIONS

Before we can have a positive impact on the bullying problem, we need to understand what bullying is—and what it isn't. Our goals for this chapter were to increase your awareness of the problem by giving a specific definition of bullying, distinguishing it from aggression and normal play, and dispelling some common myths about bullying that stand in the way of our efforts to help children. The next chapter looks at what child, family, school, community, and societal factors are associated with bullying—and what we as parents can do to respond.

CHAPTER
2

What Causes Bullying and What Can We Do?

When we conduct workshops, parents commonly ask us what causes bullying: Why do some children and adolescents bully, while others don't? The reasons one child becomes a bully and another becomes a target of bullying are complex, and why some children are accepted and supported by peers while others are rejected is difficult to determine. However, we are able to identify a number of risk and protective factors in children's lives that may play a part in whether or not they will become bullies or targets. Knowing about these factors will help you to evaluate your own family's strengths and identify any areas that may need your attention. Although some of these factors can't be controlled, it is possible to determine which ones are in your power to influence or change. We'll have some suggestions to help you determine which of these factors is within your sphere of influence to change—and to identify the resources you have to help make those changes happen.

RISK AND PROTECTIVE FACTORS

Certain risk and protective factors appear to be associated with children's engaging or not engaging in bullying behaviors. To understand how risk factors and protective factors can play a role in bullying, first consider how these types of factors relate to heart disease. We know that heart disease is associated with heredity (predisposing a person to risk), fatty diet, smoking, and lack of exercise. Protective factors also apply: heredity (predisposing a person to resilience), healthy diet, not smoking, and daily exercise. Given these risk and protective factors, can we say that smoking or a lack of exercise causes heart disease? Not really, but we can say that for each risk factor a person has, his or her likelihood of having heart-related health problems increases—in other words, these risks add up. Likewise, no single protective factor assures a person of a healthy heart, but the combination of protective factors is certainly associated with less likelihood of heart problems. The risks don't *cause* the problem, and

17

protective factors don't *prevent* the problem, but risk and protective factors do appear to *influence* the problem. Notice also that some factors are within our control (for example, whether or not we choose to smoke) and some are outside of our control (for example, genetic factors).

Risk and protective factors are also important in the bullying equation. Having more risk factors increases the likelihood that a child or adolescent will behave or respond in a negative or aggressive way to events. Again, the risk factors themselves do not cause a child to respond in a particular way. However, the greater the number of risk factors, the higher the likelihood that a child will engage in bullying behavior. Having more protective factors, on the other hand, is associated with less likelihood that a child will respond with aggression.

We all know some people who seem to have the knack of moving through relationships without many problems or conflicts. We could say that they have what they need to avoid conflicts or resolve problems when they do develop. Some families and children have greater risk factors, whereas others seem to have more protective factors. The fact that you, as a parent, are involved enough to read a book on the subject of bullying indicates that there are many positive factors operating in your family!

The risk and protective factors associated with bullying and other forms of aggression are complex—far more complex than those for the heart disease example we provided. They operate at all of the levels shown in Figure 2: the individual child, the family, the school, the community, and society.

To organize and communicate the different risk and protective factors involved in the development of bullying and other forms of aggression, we developed the listings of factors presented at the end of this chapter. The Search Institute, located in Minneapolis, Minnesota, has identified a number of *developmental assets,* similar to what we consider to be protective factors. The more assets a child has,

Figure 2   Levels of Influence on Bullying Behavior

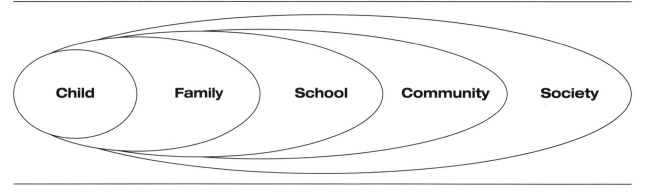

the more likely that child is to have successful outcomes in life. External assets include support, empowerment, and boundaries and expectations; internal assets include commitment to learning, positive values, social competencies, and positive identities. The grades K–5 teacher's manual for *Bully Busters* includes a more detailed explanation of the developmental assets. If you are interested, we recommend reading what we have to say there or pursuing information directly from the Search Institute (**www.search-institute.org**).

ACTIVITY 2.1

Consider the following vignettes. Although no one can predict the future for the three children we next describe, it is possible to identify some risk and protective factors just from these brief descriptions. Which ones can you identify?

José

José has always been a little small for his age. Despite this fact, he is outgoing and popular with his classmates. In addition to his smaller stature, José lacks coordination and is seldom selected when the class chooses team players during recess and other organized sports activities. Though this bothers José a little, he is able to feel good about himself because of his intellectual ability and academic success. In class, students often ask him for help on difficult assignments, and he is a popular choice on the days that the class has its weekly quiz bowl.

Risk Factors	*Protective Factors*
Small size	Popular, outgoing, confident
Uncoordinated	Good intellectual abilities/ academic success
Not selected for team sports	Students turn to him for academic help

Martha

Martha can't remember a time when she wasn't taller than her classmates. Because of her height, she has always been comfortable taking leadership roles in both sports and social activities in the classroom. Martha has always been able to stand up for herself, and she is very influential when it comes to getting her way. In fact, her behavior can be a bit abrasive and confrontational when things don't turn out as she believes they should. She is very sensitive to others' having different opinions and occasionally thinks that people disagree with her "just because." Though her concerns about others can bother her, she has found that she can make and maintain friends easily.

Risk Factors	*Protective Factors*
Physically larger than other children her age	Leader in sports and social events
Abrasive with others, confrontational	Confident, influential, sensitive
Others sometimes disagree with her	Makes friends easily

Kevin

Things have been pretty stressful in Kevin's home ever since his dad was laid off. With money being as tight as it is, worries about how to pay the rent and other bills leave little time and energy for the kids in the family. Because of their financial problems, the family rarely engages in activities they used to enjoy. In fact, it seems that the only time Mom or Dad communicates with the kids is to punish them when they are getting too loud or out of hand. Though Kevin continues to help his younger siblings with their homework most nights, his mom and dad have stopped telling him how neat they think it is that he is such a smart and helpful big brother.

Risk Factors	*Protective Factors*
Family problems, unemployment	Cares for younger siblings
Little time for family togetherness	Helps around the house
Parents very stressed out	Intelligent

ACTIVITY 2.2

Now think about how risk and protective factors might be operating in your own lives and the lives of your children:

► Read through the lists of risk and protective factors in Figures 2 through 6, on pages 24–31. Put an asterisk (*) in the first column beside any characteristics or factors that seem particularly relevant to you and your family.

- You'll notice that a blank column appears on each figure. Use this column to write any comments about how the characteristics identified relate to your own situation.

- At the end of each figure is a blank box for you to record additional notes. Describe any other factors or issues that may be operating for your child, family, school, and community—and for society as a whole.

Be sure to discuss your responses with your parenting partner and with other parents, if possible.

RECOGNIZING YOUR SPHERE OF INFLUENCE

No parent can address all the potential risk factors a child or adolescent may face related to bullying and being targeted for bullying, and it would be futile to try. It would be an exasperating waste of time to attempt to make the television, film, and music industries come together to depict healthy role models and effective problem solving. Even having them limit access to questionable material is difficult. It is also unlikely that government agencies will take on the task. There is little promise that the clothing industry is suddenly going to emphasize modesty in their clothing design or advertisements. And there is little indication that the nation will be able to completely undo the social ills of poverty.

Obviously, increasing all protective factors and reducing all risk factors is impossible. How can we respond when the problem is so enormous? We recommend a very simple solution: Start with your own *sphere of influence.* Your sphere of influence is that part of your life—and your child's—that you have the power to influence or change. You may not be able to influence a movie theater to show less violent films, but you can monitor your child to make certain he or she doesn't attend violent films. You may not be able to make all the young people in your neighborhood more honest and respectful, but you can monitor your child's involvement with individuals you think are a problem. You can definitely influence the family values you communicate to your child—and you can take steps toward making your neighborhood a safer place.

We have found that when parents don't dwell on what is beyond their sphere of influence and instead concentrate on what they *can* change, taking measures to help solve problems becomes much more manageable. If we all exert our influence in the areas we can change, we can expect to have a powerful impact on the lives of our children.

ACTIVITY 2.3

Take a look at the various areas listed in Figure 7, on page 32.

► Write down your thoughts about which aspects of your life you can and can't influence in each of the areas identified.

► Come up with some steps to take to help you make changes in the areas you can.

For this activity, it also will be important for you to discuss your responses with your parenting partner and with other parents, if possible.

IDENTIFYING AVAILABLE RESOURCES

We know that not all families are the same. Each family has its own risk and protective factors—and all families can bring their strengths to bear in creating a supportive household and helping young people stop the bullying process.

ACTIVITY 2.4

Figure 8, on page 33, identifies some of the resources families can draw on for help:

► Consider the people who might fill these roles and lend support to your own efforts to change, then add their names to the chart.

► Identify any other resources that might be of assistance in your particular situation.

Identifying familiar resources like the ones already listed is a valuable beginning. It is also important for you to identify other resources that can assist you in your particular situation—for instance, community mental health or family services. You may need to make some phone calls to find out who can help and how. Collaborating with your parenting partner or other parents is a good idea.

SUMMARY AND CONCLUSIONS

Although bullying is clearly a problem in schools and communities today, not all children bully or are targeted by bullies—in fact, the majority of children and adolescents do neither of these things. Risk and protective factors related to bullying and victimization provide some clues as to which children will become involved and how. Some families have many protective factors working for them, whereas others lack the personal, family, school, and community supports that appear to protect children from the problem. As parents, we need to determine which problems are, and are not, in our sphere of influence. In this chapter, we have suggested that it is important to know what is in our sphere of influence so that we can use all the resources available to us toward making necessary changes. The next chapter describes some tools we have found useful in our work to help enhance family bonds and support children who are involved in bullying situations.

Figure 2   Child Risk and Protective Factors

Characteristic	Risk Factor	Protective Factor	Your Child
Physical size	Small children may be picked on by bigger kids; very large children may be more aggressive or threatening.	Families teach children that size is what it is and should not lead to fear or aggression—we should accept ourselves and others as we are.	
Interpersonal style	Children who are shy, quiet, withdrawn, and easily intimidated are often picked on.	Children who make friends easily and have a positive, outgoing way about them attract others and are usually left alone by bullies.	
Problem-solving style	Some children are more abrasive and confrontational, a behavioral style that sometimes results in aggressive behavior.	Assertive children can be leaders and influential when the characteristic is combined with appropriate social skills.	
Physical aptitude	Children who lack coordination, strength, or talent for sports or other school activities may be singled out or teased.	Children who are talented at physical activities or are able to play well enough to be valued team members are more easily included in groups.	
Additional Notes			

From *A Parent's Guide to Understanding and Responding to Bullying: The Bully Busters Approach,*
© 2008 by A.M. Horne, J.L. Stoddard, and C.D. Bell. Champaign, IL: Research Press (800-519-2707; www.researchpress.com)

Figure 3 Family Risk and Protective Factors

Characteristic	Risk Factor	Protective Factor	Your Family
Family structure	Families who lack structure may be chaotic or disorganized, and children may fail to develop self-control and discipline.	Families with structure and order have closeness and predictability in family routines; children learn self-control.	
Family support	Families may be very autonomous or independent and provide little support to one another, resulting in children's seeking attention or control in aggressive ways.	Families who are tightly knit and supportive and whose members spend time nurturing one another and providing support offer greater strength against problems.	
Family finances	Families may lack the resources to provide adequately for children and adults.	Families with sufficient resources to cover the necessities and even provide extras have less stress and fewer problems.	
Family discipline	Families who are extremely punishing, overly lax, or inconsistent tend to have more discipline problems and more acting-out children, who may then bully or be bullied.	Families with clear expectations for behavior and who provide consistent and fair discipline combined with a supportive family environment, particularly when problems develop, have fewer children who bully or are bullied.	

From *A Parent's Guide to Understanding and Responding to Bullying: The Bully Busters Approach*,
© 2008 by A.M. Horne, J.L. Stoddard, and C.D. Bell. Champaign, IL: Research Press (800-519-2707; www.researchpress.com)

Figure 3 (continued)

Characteristic	Risk Factor	Protective Factor	Your Family
Family supervision	Families who provide little supervision or monitoring of child experience greater discipline problems and more rebellion.	Families engaged in and aware of their child's behavior, friends, and location, and who monitor the child's time and whereabouts, have fewer problems with their child's behavior.	
Family support of violence	Families who settle problems with coercion, violence, or revenge have children who do the same and have more problems with bullying.	Families who resolve conflict through discussion, compromise, and cooperation have better functioning families, less conflict, and fewer problems with bullying.	

Additional Notes

Figure 4 School Risk and Protective Factors

Characteristic	Risk Factor	Protective Factor	Your Child's School
Supervision of students	Teachers and schools with low supervision of students leave students vulnerable to problems, either as bullies or targets.	Children whose time and behavior is supervised have less opportunity to get into trouble and exert more self-control when they are unsupervised.	
Closeness, valuing	Students who feel a lack of closeness to their teachers and classmates are more isolated and more likely to feel alone and unsupported and to cause problems.	Students who develop a closeness with teachers and fellow students treat them with respect and friendship and engage in more cooperative behavior.	
Discipline	Schools and classrooms that provide little effective discipline or that are very punishing or unfair have unruly children, who then act as bullies.	Effective classrooms and school rules lead to students' understanding the rules and behaving appropriately; fair discipline leads to children's behaving fairly.	
Alternatives to violence	Many children lack knowledge of alternatives to violence. Teachers need to teach problem solving and conflict resolution; otherwise, students engage in aggression and violence to resolve conflict.	When students learn effective problem-solving skills and how to manage conflict, they engage in fewer bullying situations, as either bully or target.	

From A Parent's Guide to Understanding and Responding to Bullying: The Bully Busters Approach.
© 2008 by A.M. Horne, J.L. Stoddard, and C.D. Bell. Champaign, IL: Research Press (800-519-2707; www.researchpress.com)

Figure 4 (continued)

Characteristic	Risk Factor	Protective Factor	Your Child's School
Academic ability	Children with academic and learning problems have a higher likelihood of developing behavior problems.	Children who have adequate academic abilities have fewer behavior problems.	

Additional Notes

Figure 5 Community Risk and Protective Factors

Characteristic	Risk Factor	Protective Factor	Your Community
Safety/violence	Communities that have a high rate of crime and violence make children less sensitive to violence and increase children's tendency to be more aggressive.	Children in communities that implement plans for safety, have well-established plans for caring for residents, and show little tolerance for aggression are less likely to engage in aggression.	
Quality of life/services/resources	Communities that have few services and that are unable to provide adequate child care or health and safety result in children who are angry, bitter, and more likely to act out.	Communities with a good quality of life and greater resources demonstrate to children that they are cared for, resulting in less likelihood that children will act out.	
Additional notes			

From *A Parent's Guide to Understanding and Responding to Bullying: The Bully Busters Approach,*
© 2008 by A.M. Horne, J.L. Stoddard, and C.D. Bell. Champaign, IL: Research Press (800-519-2707; www.researchpress.com)

Figure 6   Society's Risk and Protective Factors

Characteristic	Risk Factor	Protective Factor	Your Comments
Violence in our culture	Cultures that are more supportive of violence have much higher rates of aggression; children exposed to violence at the local and national level accept it as appropriate behavior.	Cultures that speak out against violence and that have people who demonstrate regard for personal safety, tolerance, and respect for all people have less aggression.	
Television/movies/music	Children who are exposed to a high rate of violence on television and in movies or who hear music with violent lyrics are more likely to engage in aggression and violence against others.	When families restrict access to violent television, movies, and music or discuss problems with the content of the media with their children, they have fewer problems with aggression and violence.	
Poverty	Poverty does not cause bullying or violence, but it is associated with problems of aggression. People living in poverty are usually exposed to a high rate of violence and aggression in their community.	An adequate income provides children with the resources they need in their lives without giving them everything they want.	
Access to weapons	Children who have easy access to weapons and have weapons at school or in the community are more likely to resort to aggression and violence to resolve conflict.	Children who do not have access to weapons are more likely to learn more adaptive, socially appropriate skills for resolving conflict.	

From A Parent's Guide to Understanding and Responding to Bullying: The Bully Busters Approach,
© 2008 by A.M. Horne, J.L. Stoddard, and C.D. Bell. Champaign, IL: Research Press (800-519-2707; www.researchpress.com)

Figure 6 (continued)

Characteristic	Risk Factor	Protective Factor	Your Comments
Friends	Friends who support violence are like "birds of a feather, who flock together." When the peer group relies on violence for conflict resolution, violence becomes the only means of addressing problems. Bullies often lack alternatives to violence.	When friends treat one another with respect and resolve conflict in an effective manner, there is no need for violence and aggression.	
Additional Notes			

Figure 7   Sphere of Influence

Area	Can Influence	Cannot Influence	Steps toward Change
In the home ▲ Television and other media ▲ Family time ▲ Other			
In the neighborhood ▲ Friends ▲ Time out of the house ▲ Other			
At school ▲ Academics ▲ Behavior ▲ Other			
In the community ▲ Safety ▲ Resources and services ▲ Other			
Other areas			

From *A Parent's Guide to Understanding and Responding to Bullying: The Bully Busters Approach*,
© 2008 by A.M. Horne, J.L. Stoddard, and C.D. Bell. Champaign, IL: Research Press (800-519-2707; www.researchpress.com)

Figure 8   Helpful Resources

Resource	Contact	Type of Help	Outcome Expected
Family	Parenting partner and children, extended family _____	Figure out how much of a problem exists.	Develop better communication about understanding of the problem.
Church	Youth minister _____	See if others in the congregation are having similar concerns.	Develop group support for dealing with the problem.
School	Teacher, counselor, principal _____ _____	Find out what my child's experiences are and what the school is doing to help.	Enlist the school to be a partner with me in reducing the bullying problem.
Neighbors	Several close neighbors _____ _____	Talk about what's happening in the neighborhood related to bullying.	Have an agreement among parents that we are stopping bullying in our neighborhood.
Other resource _____	_____		

From *A Parent's Guide to Understanding and Responding to Bullying: The Bully Busters Approach,*
© 2008 by A.M. Horne, J.L. Stoddard, and C.D. Bell. Champaign, IL: Research Press (800-519-2707; www.researchpress.com)

Figure 8 (continued)

Resource	Contact	Type of Help	Outcome Expected
Other resource _____	_____ _____		
Other resource _____	_____ _____		

CHAPTER
3
Tools for Strong Families

In the last chapter, we identified risk and protective factors associated with bullying, stressed the importance for parents of knowing what is and what isn't in their sphere of influence to change, and identified a number of resources parents can look to for assistance. All children benefit from the foundation a strong family provides. This chapter describes tools that parents who participate in our Bully Busters program have found helpful for keeping their families strong. Equally valuable for children who bully and their targets, these tools include the following:

► The Family Council meeting

► The Big Questions

► Emotional intelligence and emotional coaching

► Modeling positive attitudes and behaviors

► Specific strategies for maintaining a positive relationship between parents and children

From time to time as we proceed through the book, we'll be making suggestions for using these tools. First, however, here are some basic rules for parents for keeping things positive in the family.

GUIDELINES FOR HEALTHY, HAPPY FAMILIES

Families should be inviting, not coercive. As parents, we want our children to avoid dangerous situations. Families, on the other hand, should be places where children want to be and we want them to be as well. We sometimes refer to the following guidelines for keeping families positive as the 10 "Bs":

1. Be inclusive.

Children love to be included in family discussions and activities; they want to be part of what is going on, and their desire for inclusion is very strong. We are currently working with follow-up studies of adolescents in high school, and the number one regret they voice now about their families is the lack of togetherness and closeness. Don't be hesitant to be inclusive and to make family events inviting to children.

2. Be fun.

Along with inclusion, part of the function of a healthy family is to be fun. We want our children to enjoy being with us, and this means making humor, laughter, and joy part of the experience. Being fun includes involvement and engagement, not teasing and humiliation, which some parents unfortunately think are funny. Children who are laughed at by their parents learn to laugh at others and to use teasing and ridicule as a means of interaction instead of developing healthy and happy relationships that are more mature and health promoting.

3. Be encouraging.

There are so many opportunities in life for children to become discouraged. The family should be an encouraging place to be. This type of family environment includes encouraging your child to participate in family discussions, try new ideas and activities, and take the lead in family events. The Family Council, described shortly, provides opportunities for encouragement, but even more important are daily interactions that help children feel confident, poised, and enthusiastic. The use of kind and loving words and the opportunity to play and work together lead to children's self-confidence and a sense of worth to the family.

4. Be honest.

Children are amazingly talented at detecting dishonesty, and when they experience parents who are not truthful and dependable, they take on these characteristics themselves. Answer questions children have, at the level of development that they will understand, in truthful and honest ways.

5. Be firm.

Say what you mean, and mean what you say. So often, parents use words as threats, not consistent messages, and children learn how to "manage" the parents to get their own way. We experience parents who tell their child to do or not do something, then when the child argues or has a tantrum, relent and let the child have his or her way in order to avoid conflict. Unfortunately, not following though just extends the conflict because it teaches the child that the parents don't mean what they say and will give in if coerced by the child.

6. Be NICE.

The N in NICE stands for *noticing*, whereby parents notice the good things a child does—in essence, "catching the child being good." The I stands for *increase* the times the child is being good by providing opportunities and experiences in which the child has the chance to be good. The *C* stands for *creating* time together and doing things that lead to positive social skills and interactions. The *E* refers to *encouraging* more positive social interactions by talking, modeling positive behaviors, and providing opportunities.

7. Be a source of security.

Many children experience fear, sometimes from real life and sometimes from watching television news and learning about atrocities of war, crime, gangs, and other threatening situations. They also at times experience fear related to school and community settings, particularly if bullying or other threats are part of the experience. They need to have parents who are encouraging and supportive, and who provide reassurance and comfort when problems arise.

8. Be respectful.

If we value being respected as parents, we must be respectful ourselves. This means treating children with care but expecting them to act responsibly as well. We expect our children to act in respectful and developmentally appropriate ways. We often encourage parents to treat children as they would a guest or friend: with respect. So rather than yelling at a child who inattentively tracks in muddy shoeprints, we would ask the child to stop immediately, take off the shoes, and set about correcting the situation—a respectful way to manage the problem.

9. Be a positive role model.

Our work with children over several decades has given us the personal experience to prove what research has often shown: The most powerful people in a child's life are the parents. Children observe, interact, and replicate the behaviors of parents. They learn what is acceptable and what is unacceptable through observing others. They notice the consistency of what we say and do, file away the level of honesty and fairness they see, and interact with others in the ways we modeled such interactions. In short, children learn more from us about their beliefs, values, and behaviors than from any other person.

10. Be fair.

A complaint we often hear from children when something happens is that "it isn't fair." Though they sometimes use this complaint as a delaying tactic or to see if they can get away with something, sometimes they are exactly right in their estimation. It is not fair to treat children unfairly. Children learn early on that when people with power— parents—treat others unfairly, the lesson to be learned is to be the most powerful, not the one who is fair. If we really want fairness from our children, we need to demonstrate it consistently.

THE FAMILY COUNCIL MEETING

One of the most important things family members can do is talk to one another. Of course, talking can take place in many different ways, and one particular way is by holding a Family Council meeting. The Family Council meeting is a regularly scheduled time for the whole family to meet and establish family guidelines, discuss behaviors and expectations, and make decisions. The meeting provides an opportunity for all family members to come together and identify concerns and problems, as well as to discuss areas with which they are pleased and ways to help the family function even better. As an added benefit, Family Council meetings highlight the importance of the family's setting aside time to spend together.

Here are some basic steps for getting these meetings going.

Step 1

Set up time for the meeting when all members of the family can be present. Meetings should be held regularly—if possible, once a week at a regular day and time—and should last no longer than 30 minutes.

Step 2

Get a notebook to keep notes from the meeting so that you can document issues and decisions. Find a safe place to keep the notebook in the house so you can always find it.

Step 3

Choose someone to chair the first meeting. The chair prepares a written agenda based on input from the other family members about what each would like to discuss. We suggest that an adult chair the first meeting to model effective family meeting leadership—keeping everyone on track, making sure everyone gets a chance to speak, and so forth.

Step 4

When the meeting starts, the chair reads the agenda and conducts the meeting. A time limit of three to five minutes should be enforced for each topic to ensure that meetings do not run beyond the intended 30-minute time frame. Either the chair or another member of the family can take notes from the meeting.

Step 5

Soon after the meeting, the chair takes a few minutes to write down family members' opinions of how the meeting went and what might need to be improved for the next meeting. Topics not covered during one week's meeting should go at the top of the next week's agenda.

It's a good idea for the plans and decisions made at one Family Council meeting to stay in effect until the next meeting.

ACTIVITY 3.1

Schedule a Family Council meeting to familiarize family members with the approach. Go through the meeting procedures and define a topic to be discussed. It may be good to focus initially on a simple, positive topic (for example, what to do on the weekend or where to go on vacation). Conduct the meeting according to the procedures we described.

After the meeting, ask yourself the following questions:

► Overall, how did the meeting go? Did it meet your expectations?

_____

_____

► Think about participation. Did everyone participate? If not, do you have thoughts on why? What might you do differently to have greater participation next time?

_____

_____

_____

► Were the topics interesting and relevant? Did the family take them seriously?

_____

► Was there a process for following through to be sure agreements made would be honored? If so, what is it?

_____

_____

► How would you like to change the process for the next meeting?

_____

_____

Discuss your answers to these questions with the family before you have the next Family Council meeting.

Remember to build in fun to Family Council meetings! For example, plan a positive and reinforcing activity or topic for the end of the meeting (ordering pizza, deciding on the family's evening entertainment, and so on). Many families find the first few meetings to be uncomfortable because they are not used to having them. Once the meetings have been held a few times, they become a part of family life, and members miss the experience when it doesn't take place.

THE BIG QUESTIONS

In working with families, we have found a number of parents who are quite successful in helping their children deal with problems and conflicts. They set themselves up for success in how they approach problems and in how they relate to their children, their children's teachers, and others in their lives. One way of setting up for success is to determine your sphere of influence, as described in chapter 2. Another way of doing this is to make a habit of asking what we call the "Big Questions":

1. What is your goal?
2. What are you doing?
3. Is what you are doing helping you achieve your goal?
4. If not, what can you do differently?

Both parents and children can use the Big Questions. These questions are a basic problem-solving model that helps people become clear about what their goals are, whether what they are currently doing is working, and whether other actions might be more beneficial. We encourage you to ask yourself these questions and apply them in your life, particularly when you are feeling emotional about a situation—for example, when you are talking to your child or to school staff about a bullying problem. Here is how one family used the questions.

Lee and Theresa

Lee had been getting in trouble at school; he was bringing more and more notes home indicating that he had been a discipline problem during the day. Today, when Lee's mother, Theresa, came home, she was hoping for a quiet and peaceful evening since her day at work had been anything but that. The first thing she noticed when she entered the house, however, was an envelope on the kitchen counter, addressed to her from the school. Lee had done it again—a scuffle with another boy—and the school had ordered an in-school suspension. It was clear that the next step would be a home suspension if matters didn't change soon.

Theresa began to lose it. She was furious with Lee, angry with the school, and scared about the situation because she had no idea what to do. She began screaming at Lee, who had been in his room. When he came out, she shouted at him and threatened to hurt him if this business didn't stop. He yelled at her that it wasn't his fault and slammed his door and locked it. Theresa moved toward the door to bang on it and demand that Lee open it, but instead she just sat down and cried.

After a few minutes, Theresa remembered a handout the school counselor had given her the week before when she was talking with the counselor about Lee's "infraction of the week." The handout was called "The Big Questions." Theresa began reading through the material. It asked her to respond to questions and decide how to best handle a conflict that she was experiencing. Once she calmed down a little more, Theresa responded to the questions:

What is your goal? *My goal is to get along better with Lee, to have Lee learn to behave in school, and for him to get along with other students and the teachers. My goal is to come home at night and have a peaceful evening without yelling and arguments.*

What are you doing? *I learned Lee has been in trouble again; I yelled and screamed at him, and I threatened to hurt him if this problem at school didn't stop.*

Is what you are doing helping you achieve your goal? *Not at all! In fact, it is just the opposite of what I wanted. I had a fight with Lee, I'm upset and crying, and he's mad at me. We've made no progress, and yet we're both upset.*

If not, what can you do differently? *Well, it is clear this isn't working to accomplish my goal of having Lee do well in school, get along with others and with me, and have the home be a pleasant place at night. So, what can I do differently?*

This last question can be the most difficult. Coming up with new ways of handling situations often involves changing old habits; it takes creativity, effort, and patience. Not only are you changing, but the others around you will likely resist the change, making your work harder. At the beginning, the process may be challenging, but you have probably come to the realization that "for things to change, things have to change." There really is no alternative.

Here are some thoughts about what Theresa could do differently: First, when Theresa gets bad news from school, she can spend a few minutes settling down first. She should avoid taking immediate action because she is too tired and angry. When Theresa is calm, she can talk with Lee in a confident manner. She can explain that this situation cannot go on and that they will both have to take steps to change it. Theresa could ask Lee to give her information about what happened, then explain to him that she plans to have a meeting with both the principal and the counselor, as well as any teachers involved, to get an explanation from them about the type of problems they've been experiencing and what they think can be done.

Theresa can then make an appointment with the school to go in and discuss the situation. As a part of the discussion, she can work to develop a plan of action—what is to be done by whom and when. This may involve having the teachers or the counselor prepare a "Daily Report Card," a note from the school to Theresa informing her of how Lee behaved at school that day. That way, if Lee did well, it will be possible in the evening for Theresa and Lee to spend some positive time together; if not, then the school should suggest a consequence for Lee at school, and Theresa should plan on consequences at home. At home, because Lee is consuming time and energy from Theresa in a very negative way, Lee should be expected to help make things better by working responsibly on some home projects (such as pulling weeds, doing laundry or dishes, or taking out the trash) or lose some privilege (such as television) every time he brings home a negative note from school.

Theresa could also consider making an appointment with a child specialist for some additional guidance and support. This may be through a center for religious activity; it may be on referral from the school; or it may be through a community help center or private practice counselor or therapist who specializes in helping parents with challenging children. Theresa can meet with the specialist and discuss her goals, what she is doing, the outcomes, and what she can do differently. (That's right—discuss the Big Questions!) Theresa can take some of her notes from activities or Family Council meetings along so that she will have plenty of great examples to share with the specialist. Usually the type of problem Lee is demonstrating can be addressed quickly and with minimal expense and time, but it is essential that Lee's behavior be addressed very soon because the longer it goes on, the worse the potential outcomes.

ACTIVITY 3.2

At a Family Council meeting or during other family time, discuss a problem that has come up during the week. As a family, talk through the Big Questions as they apply to the issue:

1. What is your goal?
2. What are you doing?

3. Is what you are doing helping you achieve your goal?

4. If not, what can you do differently?

It is important to ask the Big Questions in a supportive way, the goal being to clarify problems and find more effective ways of managing difficulties, not to assign blame.

Use a copy of the Big Questions Form, given as Figure 9, to write down your thoughts. Copy and use this form any time working through the questions would be helpful.

EMOTIONAL INTELLIGENCE AND EMOTIONAL COACHING

In 1990, Peter Salovey and John Mayer coined the term *emotional intelligence* to refer to the ability of a person to monitor his or her feelings, as well as the feelings of others, and to use this information to guide thinking and behavior. The concept became even more popular in 1997 when Daniel Goleman published his bestseller *Emotional Intelligence.*

As it is now generally defined, emotional intelligence involves four components:

1. Perceiving and expressing emotion—involving the ability to perceive emotions in oneself and others (as well as in objects, art, stories, music, and other stimuli)

2. Using emotion to facilitate thinking—involving emotions needed in the communication of feelings or in other cognitive processes

3. Understanding emotions—involving the ability to understand emotional information and how emotions combine and progress in relationships, as well as to appreciate emotional meanings

4. Managing emotions—the ability to be open to feelings and to modulate them in oneself and others to promote personal understanding and growth

In chapter 2, we stressed the importance of understanding the risk and protective factors related to bullying. Although many of these factors are beyond our control, emotional intelligence and awareness are factors over which families *do* have control. Children and adolescents who demonstrate high levels of emotional intelligence have lower levels of aggression and fewer behavior problems than children with lower levels of emotional intelligence. Children who are able to convey information to other people about what they are experiencing and understand what others are feeling have an enormous advantage in dealing with problems in relationships and in influencing how relationships develop. In contrast, children who do not

Figure 9   Big Questions Form

1. What is your goal?

   _____

   _____

   _____

   _____

2. What are you doing?

   _____

   _____

   _____

   _____

3. Is what you are doing helping you achieve your goal?

   _____

   _____

   _____

   _____

4. If not, what can you do differently?

   _____

   _____

   _____

   _____

From *A Parent's Guide to Understanding and Responding to Bullying: The Bully Busters Approach,*
© 2008 by A.M. Horne, J.L. Stoddard, and C.D. Bell. Champaign, IL: Research Press (800-519-2707; www.researchpress.com)

understand what others are feeling or experiencing have difficulty in social interactions and in developing meaningful relationships.

You are more likely to raise an emotionally intelligent child if you take the following steps.

Become aware of your own and your child's emotions.

In order to understand your child's emotions, you first must be aware of your own. Being aware of your own and your child's emotions does not mean being overly emotionally expressive or losing control; it means being able to identify emotions and put a name to them.

Recognize your child's emotion as an opportunity for intimacy and teaching.

Negative emotions can be made less intense by giving them a name and talking about them. Listening to your child's less intense negative emotional feelings (for instance, sadness about a broken toy) sends the message that your child can come to you when bigger problems (like bullying) occur.

Listen empathically and validate your child's feelings.

Empathy means being able to understand both what someone is saying and how they feel about what they are saying. Listening when your child talks to you and then reflecting back the feelings you hear is a very powerful bonding experience. We all like to be listened to; we can all tell when it is happening. A part of being empathic is having the ability to read your child's body language (facial expressions, posture, and so on) and remembering that your child can read your body posture as well. Are you looking your child in the eye, facing your child instead of doing other things, and paying attention? Have you turned the cell phone and television off?

Help your child find words to label the emotions she or he is having.

This process is quite different from telling children how to feel; rather, it is helping them find ways to describe the feelings they are having. The following activity can give everyone in the family some practice in learning the language of emotions.

ACTIVITY 3.3

During a Family Council meeting or other family time, look at the Feelings Chart in Figure 10, on page 48. Have each member of the family choose a feeling and talk about it or act it out. Discuss how different people can have different feelings about things and how one person can have different feelings at different times.

Afterward, think about how the activity went.

▶ What feelings did family members choose?

_____

_____

▶ Do you have additional thoughts about your family and feelings? If so, record them here.

_____

_____

_____

Parents can help their children develop emotional awareness and empathy through what we call *emotional coaching*. Whenever your child is describing an event (either positive or negative), encourage him or her to step into the experience of the other people involved. Ask questions such as "What do you think he was thinking when this happened?" "What do you think she was feeling?" and "How were *you* feeling?" The next activity can give you a start in taking on the emotional coaching role.

ACTIVITY 3.4

Watch a movie or television program with your child. Start by selecting a character your child seems to like (for example, the hero or main character). Whenever something significant happens to that character, ask your child these questions:

▶ What do you think the character is thinking?

_____

▶ What is the character feeling?

_____

▶ How would you feel if this happened to you? Why do you think you would feel this way?

_____

_____

As you notice empathy skills develop, you can ask your child to identify the thoughts and feelings of characters he or she might not necessarily identify with (for instance, a character of the opposite sex or a villain). Be sure to praise your child for engaging in the process, even if you feel that the response is not entirely accurate. It takes time and practice to develop these skills.

This activity would be great to do as a family, with everyone giving feedback on different characters in the movie or television program.

Here's how one parent applied emotional coaching to a real-life situation.

Victor

Victor came home after a really bad day. He had done poorly on a spelling test, forgotten his snack money, and gotten in trouble for arguing with some boys who were picking on him during lunch. Even before his mom asked him about his day, she could tell that he was under emotional stress, that things had not gone well. Recognizing that this was a teachable moment, Victor's mother said that he looked a little down and asked if he had had a difficult day. As Victor related the difficulties of his day, his mother indicated her sadness at his experiences and shared that those things would bother her, too. While they talked, Victor's mother casually asked Victor to identify his feelings so he would develop more insight into his emotional states, with the ultimate goal of becoming less reactive to them. Victor said that he was frustrated at his performance on the spelling test and upset about having forgotten his snack money again. Through talking openly and honestly with his mother, Victor also realized that when things like this happen, he tends to think that he is dumb and feel ashamed. Victor's mother pointed out that because of his own negative self-beliefs, when the two boys called Victor stupid, he was already primed to overreact. Though Victor was still sad after the conversation, his mother could tell that some of his stress had been alleviated through their heartfelt and supportive talk. She also knew that it would be some time before Victor would be able to recognize (and ultimately control) his emotions in moments of conflict or stress, but she was happy that they had taken these first steps together. She was surprised at how good she felt about her parenting as a result of this short but meaningful conversation with her son.

Figure 10   Feelings Chart

HAPPY

Happy

Excited

Overjoyed

SAD

Blue, unhappy

Down, defeated

Depressed

ANGRY

Annoyed, bothered

Irritated

Furious

SCARED

Nervous

Afraid

Petrified

ACTIVITY 3.5

Situation 1

Think of a situation in which you identified an opportunity for emotional coaching but feel that it probably could have gone better. Briefly describe it here, then answer the following questions.

_____

_____

_____

_____

► What was your emotional reaction to the situation?

_____

► What was your child's emotional reaction to the situation?

_____

► What got in the way of using this as an opportunity to practice your emotional coaching skills?

_____

_____

Situation 2

Identify another situation in which you not only identified an opportunity for emotional coaching, but also feel you were effective in coaching your child. Briefly describe it, then answer the following questions.

_____

_____

_____

► What was your emotional reaction to the situation?

_____

► What was your child's emotional reaction to the situation?

_____

► What was effective about your coaching in this situation, and why do you think it was effective?

_____

_____

MODELING

The behavioral principle of modeling rests on the assumption that most behavior is learned through observation. As parents, we can have tremendous influence over our children's behavior by modeling the attitudes and behaviors we wish our children to adopt. Obviously, then, it is essential that we try our hardest to demonstrate the behaviors we want our children to learn. In this next scenario, a parent who has modeled poor behavior changes gears to provide a model of better behavior. The activity that follows involves a two-step process to help you improve the behavior you model.

Lynne and Paul

Lynne's dad, Paul, walks in from a particularly difficult day at work. He realizes before he even gets a chance to sit down and relax that his daughter, Lynne, is in her room, having been sent there and told by her mom to "wait till your father gets home." Paul knows that the teacher has been having problems with Lynne because she has been engaging in bullying behaviors with other children. Learning that she was sent home with another note describing this unwanted behavior, Paul becomes frustrated and, as soon as he walks into Lynne's bedroom, begins yelling.

Later that week, Paul sits down at the kitchen table when he has the house to himself. He feels a little angry about this incident but is also embarrassed about his behavior. He remembers that everyone makes mistakes and that it is important that he is learning to change because his daughter will learn appropriate behaviors more quickly if he models them for her. So he turns from his anger and embarrassment to the task of generating more effective responses to this type of situation. He imagines what he'd like to do in the future and writes down a step-by-step plan. In Paul's case, he describes a scene in detail in which he tells Lynne, "I'm upset by this behavior and want to talk about it after I've had a chance to relax from my day at work." He also tells her to think about why she did what she did so that when they have this conversation they will be able to figure out what went wrong and come up with better ways of handling the situation in the future. Paul also knows that when that conversation is over, he will follow through by grounding Lynne for the weekend.

ACTIVITY 3.6

Step 1

Identify an interaction you have had with your child in which you may have modeled behavior you wish you hadn't. Describe it briefly here.

_____

_____

_____

► *Why did you act in a way that you wish you had not?* Was it habit, early learning from watching your own parents, or being tired from a busy day? It is important not to dwell on feeling guilty about earlier mistakes, but to focus energy on developing a new plan: Problem solving is much better than problem guilt.

_____

_____

Step 2

Generate a specific example of how you will choose to respond in the future when confronted with a similar situation.

_____

_____

_____

► *With your new plan, what is your goal?* Specifically, what will you be doing differently to make certain the new behavior, rather than the old behavior you are trying to change, occurs?

_____

_____

▶ *How will you know whether or not your plan is working?* It is important to remember that you can influence others by changing your own behavior. If you want respectful behavior from your child, you must model that type of behavior before explaining that you will not tolerate disrespectful behavior from your child.

_____

_____

Step 3

Try out your plan!

Step 4

Afterward, ask yourself how the plan worked. If it didn't work, what could you do differently next time?

_____

_____

_____

MAINTAINING A POSITIVE RELATIONSHIP WITH YOUR CHILD

The most practical and powerful tool you have to help your child is your relationship. Children who feel respected and valued not only feel good about themselves, they also learn to respect and value others. This, of course, positively affects children's social experiences and has ripple effects into other areas of their lives, including how well they do in school and in later life.

Some important elements of that relationship will assist you if your child engages in bullying behaviors or is the target of such behaviors. These elements include balancing support and firmness, creating an open-door policy, making a commitment to helping your child, and resolving conflicts peacefully.

Balancing Support and Firmness

Balancing support and firmness is one of the most difficult and universal challenges of parenting. Whether your child is learning to tie her shoes or relate in a positive way to her peers without conflict, balancing support and firmness is no easy matter. When you teach a child to tie her shoes, it is easy to see that if you provide too much support—always tying her shoes when she becomes frustrated—she will never have the opportunity to challenge herself, nor will she have the experience of mastering the new task. If you provide too little support—not teaching your child the basic steps in tying a shoe or giving her encouragement when she learns each of those steps—she will likely have too little information, feel that the task really doesn't matter, or both.

Keeping the Door Open

Also essential in responding to bullying situations is creating an environment in which your child feels comfortable discussing problems and concerns—bullying situations included. Keeping the door open is not an easy task. In so many of our relationships, including our relationships with our children, there are topics we would prefer not to discuss. However, for true change to occur, your child must feel free to share his experiences without risk of punishment.

If you maintain an open-door policy, permitting your child to feel safe coming to you to talk about minor events, your child is more likely to talk to you about difficult or embarrassing situations. For your child to learn from events involving bullying, it is vital that he be able to think about and discuss these events openly when they happen.

Making a Commitment

To achieve any goal, you need commitment. Spending time and effort working to improve your relationship with your child communicates your commitment. By reading this book, you are demonstrating commitment to help your child deal with bullying in a positive way. Every time you follow through with one of the activities suggested, you are showing your child that you care about what happens to her in a bullying situation.

Resolving Conflicts Peacefully

Most people believe that conflict is a negative thing, but conflict is a natural occurrence. The outcome of conflict can be good, bad, or neutral, and positive conflict resolution can lead to personal growth, learning, and change. Unresolved conflicts will not go away—they will reappear and may escalate into serious aggression or violence.

Sometimes parents get stuck in a *conflict cycle* with their child. Understandably, a conflict cycle is difficult to break because of the stubborn nature of the behaviors involved. The following example is of a common conflict cycle. Though each step might not always be present, most typical conflict cycles involve this process.

1. Your child misbehaves in a small way. You warn your child but decide not to follow through with a consequence.

2. Your child becomes more disruptive, and you find yourself becoming more frustrated.

3. You repeat the warning but do not follow though, and your child's behavior becomes worse.

4. Your child thinks that he or she has "gotten away with it."

5. You become angry, lose control of your temper, and find yourself yelling at your child.

6. Your child responds to your outburst by reducing the behavior but begins to build up resentment toward you.

7. Your child eventually engages in the smaller disruptive behavior again. This time, you recognize that the behavior becomes worse more quickly because the limits and consequences are not clear.

8. You get angry again. This time, you find that your child is more openly disrespectful and defiant.

9. You enact punishment for your child's behavior, perhaps by enforcing severe consequences.

This conflict cycle may sound very familiar to you. We have certainly heard about it many times in our parent groups. Some of the details may differ based upon your experience, but because a conflict cycle is very easy to get into, it is important to recognize and break the cycle at the beginning.

ACTIVITY 3.7

The next time you find yourself in a conflict with your child, consider whether your own and your child's actions are part of a conflict cycle. Ask yourself the following questions:

▶ First, what is the conflict about?

_____

_____

▶ Is my child's behavior escalating? If so, how?

_____

_____

▶ Are the consequences I'm giving following right along and becoming more extreme? If so, in what way?

_____

_____

▶ How can I interrupt the conflict cycle?

_____

_____

Do your best to end the cycle by stopping and thinking before you act out of anger and following through with appropriate consequences.

This isn't easy, so keep practicing and remember to keep asking the Big Questions! If conflict cycles are common, making them the subject of a Family Council meeting may help.

SUMMARY AND CONCLUSIONS

Parents and other family members have a tremendous influence on the behaviors of children, including their role in bullying situations. To keep families strong, this chapter described the Family Council meeting, an especially valuable kind of gathering in which family members come together, identify and deal with concerns, and discuss ways to help the family function even better. To help you develop new ways of understanding and responding to your child's problems, we introduced the Big Questions problem-solving model. We also discussed steps in raising an emotionally intelligent child and gave suggestions for emotional coaching. Finally, we pointed out the importance of modeling positive attitudes and behaviors, and described some key aspects of maintaining a positive relationship with your child.

References

Goleman, D. (1995). *Emotional intelligence: Why it can matter more than IQ.* New York: Bantam Books.

Salovey, P., & Mayer, J. M. (1990). Emotional intelligence. *Imagination, Cognitions, and Personality, 9,* 189–191, 193, 195, 198–200.

CHAPTER 4

Understanding Children Who Bully

In the last chapter, we gave some guidelines for healthy, happy families and described tools for strong families: the Family Council meeting, the Big Questions, emotional intelligence and coaching, modeling of positive behaviors and attitudes, and specific strategies for maintaining a good relationship with your child. This chapter focuses on children who bully. It describes different types of bullying, looks at two special cases of bullying—sexual harassment and cyberbullying—and describes the differences between boys and girls as far as bullying is concerned.

TYPES OF BULLYING

In the last few decades, research attempting to understand those who bully and their behaviors has suggested that there are three distinct types of bullying: aggressive, passive, and relational. In the following discussion, we will describe these types and take a look at two forms of bullying that are of increasing concern: sexual harassment and cyberbullying.

Aggressive Bullying

John

It is an unseasonably warm day in early March, and Ms. Peterson has decided to reward her students by taking them outside for recess following lunch. John, a fifth grader, is on the playground with his classmates in the middle of a fun but competitive game of kickball. John is toward the back of the line, waiting for a turn to kick the ball.

Hot from the sun and knowing that his team has two outs, John is becoming increasingly frustrated at the thought of not having one more chance at home plate before recess is over. He begins to fidget and dance around on his feet, having trouble keeping his hands to himself. He intentionally begins bumping into the others in line around him. Though the other students don't like this, they know they had better not push John back or make such a fuss that Ms. Peterson will notice.

Mitch, one of the smaller boys in the class, has his turn at the plate. He's gotten two strikes and has become worried now that he hears John and some of the other students taunting him, threatening him not to strike out. Unfortunately, this last pitch has been rolled with quite a bit of force and is particularly bouncy. Mitch's heart sinks when he misses his kick. He has a good idea of what is coming next.

Just as John's team is taking the outfield, Ms. Peterson blows the whistle. Recess is over, and everyone must line up. Ms. Peterson is standing by the door, talking to one of the students as the rest of the class excitedly forms a line. Shielded from Ms. Peterson's view, and with the support of a few of his friends, John continues to taunt and threaten Mitch.

With the line formed, Ms. Peterson turns and walks through the door, and the class follows. When she is well inside the building, out of sight and earshot, John pushes Mitch to the ground very hard. He stands over Mitch, calls him a bad name, and lets him know that there will be more of the same once school is out for the day.

This example is typical of aggressive bullying, the most common type overall and the most common among boys especially. John exerts control over Mitch through Mitch's expectation of harm, then actually pushes Mitch and threatens him with more punishment later. Aggressive bullies may be more physically developed than their peers and often use their size and strength to coerce and intimidate others. The scenario shows two kinds of aggressive bullying: physical aggression (the push) and verbal aggression (the taunts and threats).

Aggressive bullies are not afraid of using their strength or abilities to intimidate other students; in fact, they enjoy and take pride in their ability to dominate others. They generally do not bully in front of adults—one reason adult presence is crucial in reducing bullying—but they do often enjoy the audience that builds when they bully a weaker individual.

Here are some characteristics of aggressive bullies:

► Initiate overt aggression, or aggression that is out in the open.

► Have learned that bullying has payoffs.

► Are fearless, impulsive, and coercive.

- Are adaptable and use multiple forms of violence.
- Want to dominate others.
- Have little empathy for others.
- See the world with a "paranoid eye."

Let's examine these characteristics in more depth.

Aggressive bullies initiate overt aggression, or aggression that is out in the open.

Due to their interest in developing and maintaining a reputation that is largely anchored in fear and intimidation, aggressive bullies often seek to demonstrate their power and status by performing their bullying acts in front of a large audience. Not only does this provide the bully with the social reward of attention, it also sends a clear signal to the bystanders that "you could be next, so stay out of it."

Children who engage in aggressive bullying have learned that it has payoffs.

At times, people ask why some children would want to bully others. An answer: Why wouldn't they? In spending literally hundreds of hours with children who bully, we have heard over and over that they expect to be successful in their efforts. They have found that other children can be victimized and that physical bullying can result in prestige, power, influence, control, and other payoffs—such as lunch money. Through experience, they have learned that they probably won't get into trouble and, if they do, that the trouble they are in is probably worth whatever it is that they stand to gain by bullying.

Aggressive bullies generally are fearless, impulsive, and coercive.

Instead of being able to resolve conflicts peacefully, aggressive bullies are fearless; instead of engaging in planning and decision making, they are impulsive. And instead of being caring, they are coercive, using force or the threat of force to get others to do what they want. In short, aggressive bullies either do not possess or do not use the relational skills necessary to be reflective and caring.

Aggressive bullies are adaptable and use multiple forms of violence and threats, adapting their aggression to the situation.

Bullying may take the form of hitting, kicking, and other physical aggression—or the threat of any of these. It may also include convincing others to join in the bullying or creating gangs or cliques to carry out aggression. Aggressive bullies also damage or steal the property of other students, sometimes using force. They are adept at finding places to be aggressive and are able to create fear in their targets through subtle looks and actions. These bullies are well known and have well-deserved reputations among other students and often even school staff.

Aggressive bullies want to dominate others.

Aggressive bullies have a strong drive to be in control of others and the situation. They want to be powerful and influential, and they use their size, strength, or other superior characteristics to do so. They are easily irritated when they do not get their way, and their frustration can lead them to attempt to control weaker students. Sometimes aggressive bullies will openly attack those they target. At other times, if the opportunity presents itself, aggressive bullies will taunt or isolate their targets. Either form of aggression serves to give the bully the advantage over the target.

Aggressive bullies have little empathy for others.

Think of people you know and truly care about, and then imagine how it would feel to be cruel to them. The ability to put yourself in another person's shoes is empathy. It is very difficult to be cruel to people when we care about them, understand how they feel, and realize that they may be hurt by our actions. When children develop empathy—the ability to feel what others are feeling—it's not easy for them to be mean to others. Most children who bully others have little empathy for those they target. In fact, they are more likely to view their targets with contempt, anger, and disdain. These perceptions allow children who bully to feel that their targets deserve what they get.

Children who engage in aggressive bullying see the world with a "paranoid eye."

Aggressive bullies look at the world with suspicion. They tend to interpret negative events—such as being bumped in the hallway or having someone go ahead of them in the lunch line—as being intentional insults. If a well-adapted child is bumped in the hallway, that child is likely to assume it was an accident and ignore it. If the aggressive child is bumped, he or she immediately assumes that the bump was on purpose and that it warrants "getting even." Accidental slights are very unsettling to aggressive bullies because they threaten these children's reputations and disturb their sense of control. Unfortunately, these accidents all too often cause the aggressive bully to respond angrily and without thinking.

ACTIVITY 4.1

Reflect on your own past experiences and identify a situation of aggressive bullying that you may have witnessed or been directly involved in. Use this situation or an example from this chapter to begin a discussion with your child about this type of bullying at school. After sharing your experience, encourage your child to describe an incident of aggressive bullying.

► What happened in the incident your child describes?

_____

_____

► In addition to asking what happened, ask how your child felt and how he or she thinks the bully and target felt.

_____

_____

► Was the problem solved? If so, how? If not, how could it be solved?

_____

_____

_____

You could make this and the next two activities part of a Family Council meeting or other family time, if you wish. Other family members are likely to have much to add!

Passive Bullying

Peter

The mornings have gotten cooler now that fall is turning into winter. The high school students hang together and smoke their cigarettes before the first bell rings. Peter, a junior, is excitedly telling the others about a party he went to that weekend. Some listen actively, while others, uninterested, watch the other students walk to the building from the parking lot. Peter is hoping that his story will impress Brandon, who is known to be one of the tough guys in the school. Just at that moment, one of the approaching students, Michael, catches the attention of the group.

Michael, who is shy and socially awkward, becomes nervous as he realizes he is going to have to pass by Brandon, Peter, and the others. As Michael draws closer, Peter begins to insult his clothing and laughs loudly and purposefully. At this point, Brandon has repositioned himself so that he is now blocking the door, forcing Michael to endure Peter's remarks. Knowing that he now has everyone's attention, Peter increases the cruelty of his insults.

Passive bullying behavior is slightly less common than aggressive bullying behavior. In this type, smaller, weaker individuals use their relationship with aggressive bullies to gain attention and acceptance from their peers. In this case, Peter, who is a passive bully, wants to be accepted by the others in the group, particularly the more influential Brandon, but Peter lacks the skills to be influential among the group without resorting to being demeaning to or bullying others, which gets the attention of the group. Passive bullies are generally "going along" because they want to be recognized and be part of the group, but they lack the abilities to be a leader. In his desire to be recognized by Brandon, Peter is willing to humiliate Michael, even though he would be quite unlikely to do this independently.

Here are some characteristics of passive bullies:

► Use covert (indirect) aggression.
► Are dependent, insecure, and anxious.
► Lack strong inhibitions against aggression.
► Commonly use social exclusion.
► Participate in but do not initiate aggression.
► Lack social status among their peers.
► Act as "camp followers" or "hangers-on."

Passive bullying involves the use of covert, or indirect, aggression.

Passive bullies are more timid than aggressive bullies in their use of physical aggression. They prefer more indirect means, such as talking negatively about a person, taking property, messing up an unattended locker or desk, leaving cruel or nasty notes, or using the Internet or text messaging to send threatening messages. Though often not physical, the behaviors of the passive bully still cause significant emotional distress in their targets.

Passive bullies are generally dependent, insecure, and anxious.

These children are insecure and unsure of themselves—and are more anxious and tense than aggressive bullies. As a result, they are less apt to engage their victims in a direct fashion, though they certainly derive pleasure from displays of aggression by others. They often wait for an event to occur and join in after it has begun.

Passive bullies lack strong inhibitions against aggression.

Unlike children who do not engage in bullying behavior, passive bullies seem to lack the mechanism that keeps them from bullying. This lack of inhibition may be the result of the influence of a family that supports coercive or aggressive means of resolving conflicts. In this case, passive bullies may come to enjoy seeing aggression when they are not themselves the target of it.

Social exclusion is common among passive bullies.

Passive bullies will often encourage others to prevent someone from sitting with them at lunch or refuse to allow someone to be on their team at recess or in games. They will also give support to someone else who excludes unpopular peers from classroom or social events and join in with others who are making physical threats.

Passive bullies participate in but are unlikely to initiate aggression.

Children who engage in passive bullying are often afraid of physical confrontation, feeling they may not be as successful as the aggressive bully. In addition, they fear being caught, reprimanded, or punished. Because of these fears, passive bullies are often more responsive than aggressive bullies to interventions that teach them effective ways to resolve conflicts.

Children who engage in passive bullying lack social status among their peers.

Aggressive bullies often have high social status because others see them as having influence (even if it is a negative influence) and physical power. The passive bully is not generally recognized by his or her peers as having independent influence; without the support of other bullies, the passive bully lacks influence and social status.

Passive bullies are "camp followers" and "hangers on."

Passive bullies almost never threaten others unless they are in the presence of an aggressive bully. However, when a group of potentially aggressive kids gathers, passive bullies feel empowered to act. They have learned that they can improve their social status by having strong relationships with aggressive bullies. Because they have experienced social rewards from bullying others, they pay close attention to the actions of aggressive bullies and are quick to follow their lead.

Share an example of passive bullying from your personal experience or from this chapter, then encourage your child to describe an incident of passive bullying.

► What happened in this incident?

_____

_____

► In addition to asking what happened, ask how your child felt and how he or she thinks the bully and target felt.

_____

_____

► Was the problem solved? If so, how? If not, how could it be solved?

_____

_____

_____

Relational Bullying

Tanisha

The school year had started off well. A number of students had become friends during the beginning of the year, sat together at lunch, and spent time together after school. One day, Kathleen made a comment to Tanisha that she really enjoyed school this year but wished that Tanisha would be less critical of others. Tanisha became infuriated.

That night, Tanisha called the other girls who were part of the group and said that Kathleen had been telling stories about the other girls and didn't deserve to be a member of their group. Tanisha also said that if they continued to be friends with Kathleen, Tanisha would not be friends of theirs anymore. Since they had known Tanisha longer than Kathleen, and since Tanisha held such a strong leadership role in their group, they all agreed to exclude Kathleen from the group.

The next day, when Kathleen walked up to the group, they turned away and walked into their classrooms. At lunch, they filled the table with their group and a few other students so there would be no room for Kathleen to join them. That night, when Kathleen called several of the friends, they said they couldn't talk right then and hung up. It didn't take Kathleen long to get the message: She was not a part of the group. She had been purposefully excluded.

Kathleen was very hurt and angry. The next day, she started yelling at Tanisha about how mean she was. Tanisha just laughed and walked away, telling the other girls to ignore the weakling, who had to resort to yelling and crying—she wasn't worthy of being a friend. A teacher heard Kathleen yelling at Tanisha and gave Kathleen a detention for causing trouble. Kathleen continued to be ignored by the group for the next several weeks.

In this example, it is clear that Tanisha very intentionally isolated Kathleen and had control over how others responded to Kathleen. With her superior role as leader of the group, Tanisha was able to persuade the other girls to side with her. Finally, Tanisha made certain that the girls continued to exclude Kathleen.

Here are some characteristics of relational bullies:

▶ Among girls, are the most common type.

▶ Attempt to gain power, prestige, and influence through the exclusion of others.

▶ Try to get even when they think they have been slighted or insulted.

▶ Achieve their goals by manipulating social patterns.

▶ Spread rumors and lie to exclude others or get them in trouble.

Among girls, relational bullying is the most common type.

As we have said, aggressive bullying is the most common type of bullying among boys. With girls, bullying is more often relational and therefore more difficult to detect. Although boys engage in relational aggression to some degree, this type of bullying is usually girl against girl.

Relational bullies attempt to gain power, prestige, and influence by excluding others.

When one person excludes another from a friendship group out of "meanness," the person doing the excluding is demonstrating a level of power and influence over the person being excluded, as well as over the others in the group. This type of bully obtains a certain level of prestige as leader and manager of others' feelings and interactions.

Relational bullies try to get even when they think they have been slighted or insulted.

Those who engage in relational bullying use exclusion to get even with someone who has slighted or insulted them—or with someone they perceive as having slighted or insulted them. Tanisha turned the group against Kathleen because she had criticized Tanisha. The exclusion was a means of getting even for an insult Tanisha only perceived. Actually, Kathleen was attempting to be constructive and meant no harm. Tanisha's response was disproportionate and unbalanced, an example of viewing the world through a paranoid eye.

Relational bullies manipulate social patterns.

All children enjoy feeling influential and powerful. However, relational bullies attempt to achieve their goals—for influence, power, or material gains—by causing conflict or alliances among others.

Relational bullying often involves rumors or lies.

It is common for children who engage in relational bullying to spread rumors or lies about others. Generally, our experience with relational bullies is that they feel little remorse; in fact, they often congratulate themselves on being able to get someone in trouble or damage the reputations and relationships of others.

A concern of many parents and counselors is associated with the fact that relational bullies excel at understanding the problems and feelings of others, a component of being empathic. Rather than using their understanding to help others, however, relational bullies use it to hurt or disparage. For example, a relational bully may appear to be quite empathic, listening compassionately as a friend describes a particularly troublesome matter, such as considering having sex with a boyfriend or a parent's unemployment, but then spread the news among others, sometimes through the Internet. While this may not be an issue for your child, it is something to keep in mind.

ACTIVITY 4.3

Share an example of relational bullying from your personal experience or from this chapter, then encourage your child to describe an incident of relational bullying.

► What happened in this incident?

▶ In addition to asking what happened, ask how your child felt and how he or she thinks the bully and target felt.

_____

_____

▶ Was the problem solved? If so, how? If not, how could it be solved?

_____

_____

_____

SEXUAL HARASSMENT AND CYBERBULLYING

Two special cases—sexual harassment and cyberbullying—deserve mention. Strictly speaking, a single incident of either of these events wouldn't be considered bullying. However, sexual harassment and cyberbullying often *do* fit the PIC criteria. These acts can be purposeful (P), represent an imbalance of power (I), and continuous (C)—and both forms are of increasing concern.

Sexual Harassment

People are often confused about what constitutes sexual harassment and whether sexual harassment is bullying. The U.S. Equal Opportunity Commission defines sexual harassment this way:

> Unwelcome sexual advances, requests for sexual favors, and other verbal or physical conduct of a sexual nature constitute sexual harassment when this conduct explicitly or implicitly affects an individual's employment, unreasonably interferes with an individual's work performance, or creates an intimidating, hostile, or offensive work environment.

While this definition concerns adults in the workplace, it fits schools because it emphasizes the unwelcome nature of the advances and includes the ideas that they can be physical or verbal and that they interfere with a person's ability to work. In the case of students, that would mean interfering with academic and social tasks related to school. In our experience, sexual harassment in schools usually meets the PIC criteria: It is purposeful, there is an imbalance of power, and it occurs more than once. Any school that does not attend to the problem is not providing a safe environment for young people. School personnel must address sexual harassment as it applies to all students, including both cross-gender harassment (male on female or female on male) and same-sex harassment. Responses are appropriate when children use derogatory sexual names or disparage someone's sexual orientation.

Many see sexual harassment as different from and more serious than simple bullying. They consider all forms of sexual harassment to be violence, just as pulling a gun or a knife on another student is violence, warranting legal action. We see sexual harassment as being on a continuum, in the same way other forms of aggression are on a continuum. At a certain point, the level of aggression in an incident of sexual harassment may indeed warrant legal action.

We have worked with schools that wanted to include the problem in their bullying prevention programs, mostly middle schools, and we have worked with schools that were clear that the problem was not to be addressed as part of a program for young people. We think it is a mistake not to address this issue. Children and adolescents are involved in and aware of issues of sexuality, and we feel it is necessary for them to learn respect and dignity for all people as they relate to sexual behavior.

Cyberbullying

Keeping pace with the increasing use of technology, cyberbullying, or bullying via the Internet and through personal digital devices like cell phones and PDAs, is becoming more of a problem. The following situation is typical.

Marti

Marti had been part of a group of girls who had been friends, but when Marti and Ella both showed interest in the same boy, Jesse, sparks began to fly. Their school had a strict policy on bullying, and so the two knew it would be unwise to engage in conflict at school. When Ella got home, though, she instant messaged Marti, calling her a bitch and a slut for attempting to win Jesse as a boyfriend. Not to be outdone, Marti was quick to respond with her own instant messaging of insults. When Ella received the responses, she escalated the conflict by going to an Internet chat room that many in the school used. In the chat room, she said that Marti had been engaging in sex with several boys and shared personal information that Marti had shared previously with her. When Marti began receiving contacts from others in the chat room, soliciting sex and teasing her about the intimacies shared by Ella, she became very depressed. She felt so disgraced that she thought she could never go to school again and that there was no reason to live.

According to Nancy Willard, author of *Cyberbullying and Cyberthreats,* cyberbullying is a particularly severe form of aggression because it follows children and adolescents into their homes, even into their bedrooms. The problem isn't confined to schoolyards or classrooms, or to daytime hours. It can be happening 24/7 in chat rooms, instant messages, blogs, and online journals, places rarely supervised by adults. Bullies are able to abuse their targets without face-to-face interaction—making it possible for the abuse to be even more cruel and insensitive.

One reason it is crucial for parents to have good, open communication with their children is that, without a foundation of openness, when children are bullied they may fear their parents will become angry, tell them to figure out what to do on their own, or embarrass them when talking to teachers and other school personnel. With cyberbullying, the problem is compounded. Most children and adolescents assume that their parents don't understand the Internet and text-messaging world and fear that they won't understand cyberbullying or take it seriously or will simply take the devices away as a quick solution. They may also not want their parents knowing the Web sites they visit and fear losing access if their parents really do know what's going on.

As a result of these concerns, most children and adolescents do not tell their parents if they experience cyberbullying. A national program developed to assist schools and families with Internet safety, iSafe (**www.isafe.org**) reported that while almost all parents were confident they knew what their children were doing online, more than 40 percent of the students said they were certain their parents had no idea what sites they were using.

One of the first steps parents should take regarding cyberbullying is to discuss Internet safety in general with their children. This topic is beyond our scope here, but useful guides for parents and children are readily available on the iSafe Web site, sponsored by the U.S. Office of Juvenile Justice and Delinquency, as well as on other sites, both public and private. (See the list of resources at the back of this book for more good ideas.) Making discussion of Internet activities part of the weekly Family Council meetings can be very influential in helping young people maneuver their way safely through the Web.

The simple action of placing the computer in the family room or kitchen area, where its use is public rather than private, also can do a great deal to increase children's safety.

Regardless of where the computer is, parents should become aware of how their children are behaving after having used the computer. If a child is upset after accessing the Internet, parents should investigate further. Other warning signs of cyberbullying are the same as for children who are targets of other types of bullying:

► Drop in grades

► Withdrawal

► Aggression, despite previously being accepting and sociable

► A tendency to skip lunch or recess

► Avoidance of what would otherwise be seemingly fun activities

► Frequent trips to the nurse's office or school rest room

► Frequent complaints of illness and requests to stay home from school

► Poor sleep, nervousness, anxiety

Parents should let their children know that they take the threat of cyberbullying very seriously. If parents learn that cyberbullying is occurring, they should take immediate steps to provide support and encouragement. They should also save all evidence of cyberbullying on the computer and also on printed copies—never erase it or delete it. Once parents have the information, they can share it with the school, police, and the Internet service provider, who may take steps to identify the offender and block that person's Internet access or contact them regarding privacy and security issues.

Many schools are taking the initiative to address the problem of cyberbullying. While just a few years ago school counselors were largely unfamiliar with Internet, today many are prepared to assist parents and their children with the problem. If this isn't the case in your school, then you can encourage your school administration to become more current in their knowledge. This problem will only be expanding in the coming years.

DIFFERENCES BETWEEN GIRLS AND BOYS

There are clear differences in how girls and boys bully. Male bullies are more likely to be "equal opportunity offenders"—they will bully both girls and boys, whereas girls are more likely to focus on other girls. Table 2 includes some additional differences.

Table 2   Bullying Differences between Girls and Boys

Characteristic	Girls	Boys
Label	Usually called *mean* or similar labels; parents and educators usually do not use the term *bully* when describing girls.	Called *bullies* by parents and teachers, with no concern about stigmatizing or hurting feelings.
Direct aggression	Engage in less direct or visible aggression; more likely to use relational aggression as a way of managing conflicts or gaining power and prestige, including gossip, rumors, slandering, and exclusion.	Engage in direct and visible physical bullying, including pushing, shoving, threatening. Generally public about their aggression.
Target of aggression	Usually other girls.	Either girls or boys.
Extent of bullying	Exposed to less bullying.	Exposed to more bullying.
Age of bully	Girls tend to be bullied by girls their own age.	Majority of bullying is committed by older boys.
Frequency	Girls bully and are bullied less frequently than boys, although rates are increasing.	Boys engage in four times as much bullying as girls and are the victims of bullying twice as often.
Sexual harassment	Girls tend to be the targets of sexual harassment at a much higher rate then boys.	Boys tend to engage in sexual harassment more than girls.

In the last few years, the differences in male and female victims have become less distinct, with more girls engaging in overt physical aggression and more boys engaging in relational aggression. We have found this to be particularly true in private schools, where all the students know that physical aggression will cause them to be expelled from the school, but where relational aggression (in the form of teasing, spreading rumors, social exclusion, and put-downs) is harder to see and often goes unpunished.

SUMMARY AND CONCLUSIONS

In this chapter, we described the three types of bullying: aggressive, passive, and relational. We also noted the problems caused by sexual harassment and cyberbullying and explained the ways in which children engage in bullying behaviors. We observed that both boys and girls can and do employ all of the types of bullying described, but that boys more commonly engage in aggressive bullying, whereas girls most frequently engage in relational bullying. Now that you know about the different types of bullying, it's time to consider the focus of the next chapter—targets of bullying behaviors.

References

U.S. Equal Employment Opportunity Commission. *Sexual harassment.* Retrieved October 4, 2007, from the EEOC Web site: **www.eeoc.gov/types/sexual_harassment.html**

Willard, N. E. (2007). *Cyberbullying and cyberthreats: Responding to the challenge of online social aggression, threats, and distress.* Champaign, IL: Research Press.

Understanding Targets of Bullying

In the last chapter, we illustrated the similarities and differences among types of bullies and described some differences in the way boys and girls bully. Children who are targeted by bullies are also of different types. This chapter looks at the similarities and differences among these types of targets. We pay particular attention to the targets of relational bullying and to bystanders—a group often not considered to be victimized by the bullying experience.

TYPES OF TARGETS

As is true for children who engage in bullying behaviors, there are considerable differences among types of targets. Targets generally fall into one of the following categories: passive, provocative, and relational. Although children who witness bullying— bystanders—are not directly involved in bullying situations, we consider them to be targets as well.

Passive Targets

In chapter 4, we described a situation in which Mitch, one of the smaller boys in a fifth-grade class, was unsuccessful at kickball and as a result was targeted by John, who pushed him down and threatened him after the game. Kids like Mitch are the ones we most often have in mind when we think of targets of bullying, and they are the type most often depicted in the media.

Colin

Colin moved into his sixth-grade class at his new school mid-year. He wasn't smaller than other kids, but wasn't bigger either. Colin had never been outgoing and had always had difficulty making new friends, in part because his family moved often and each time he was the "outsider." He always dreaded starting fresh in school and usually tried to be as invisible as possible so others wouldn't bother him. Though he would like to have friends and be part of an "in-crowd," he had decided it just wasn't to be and so stayed pretty much to himself.

Toward the end of the first week, Carmen, a classmate, came over during lunch and began talking to him about where he had come from and whether he liked the new school. Colin found it really nice that someone had reached out to him and started a conversation. He was quite happy about his new acquaintance.

That afternoon, Robert and several other boys stopped Colin and told him to mind his own business and to stop talking with Carmen and other girls in the school. They said that he didn't belong there and that they would hurt him if he tried to be friends with any of the girls. Colin was distraught about the confrontation. Over the weekend, he told his mother about what had happened, and she laughed it off, saying, "All boys are jealous of new students. They were probably just teasing—don't take it so seriously."

The next week, Colin was met at school by Robert, who said, "Remember what I told you" and sneered at Colin as he walked away. Later, at lunch, Carmen again came up and said hello and talked to Colin about a trip she had taken the past weekend with her parents. Colin enjoyed talking with her but saw Robert's friends watching and became apprehensive about what would happen later.

After school, Robert came rushing up to Colin and shoved Colin to the ground and kicked him hard. Robert said, "I told you to stay away from the girls in our school. You don't belong here, and they don't want you bothering them." Colin became teary eyed, and the other boys started laughing at him and calling him names, and one even kicked dirt on Colin.

After they left, Colin began thinking of what he could do about the problem. It seemed to him that his mother wasn't going to do anything, and none of the other students seemed to be available to help him. As he walked home, he considered refusing to go to school any more, trying to find a way to defend himself with a knife or some other weapon, or . . . but he had no good ideas.

The next day, Colin was called into the counselor's office. Ms. Sherrard told Colin that he had been seen in an encounter with Robert and others yesterday, and that she needed to be sure that Colin knew the rules about not fighting at school—that anyone involved in a fight would be suspended, with no exceptions. She told Colin he had been warned and should be careful to avoid conflicts with other students. When Colin attempted to explain the situation, Ms. Sherrard stopped him and said, "I know it can be difficult being a new student in school, but it is still your responsibility to avoid conflict, and I can assure you that if you continue to be in altercations with Robert and others, there will be consequences, including in-school or out-of-school suspension."

Colin felt even more trapped, confused, and scared than he had before, for now he was being harassed by fellow students and being held accountable for any conflicts. What a mess.

When we talk about passive targets, we don't mean that these individuals passively accept their fate. What we mean is that, like Colin, they aren't actively doing anything that contributes to their victimization and they have little responsibility for the outcome. They are "just there" when the bully decides to tease, taunt, harass, or become physically aggressive. To some degree, what happens to them is a case of being in the wrong place at the wrong time. They certainly are not passive in their response to bullying: They feel threatened, scared, denigrated, humiliated, defenseless, and very vulnerable. They also share these characteristics:

- ► Generally have low self-esteem.
- ► Describe their experience as one of social isolation and abandonment.
- ► Tend to be smaller and have less developed physical skills.
- ► May be targeted because of different intellectual abilities.
- ► May be of lower socioeconomic status.
- ► Appear more anxious, nervous, and insecure than their peers.

Passive targets generally have low self-esteem.

In a general sense, passive targets have low self-esteem and, as such, may be prone to seeing themselves as failures or as deficient or defective people, unworthy of others' protection or support.

These targets describe their experience as one of social isolation and abandonment.

Social isolation is typical for this type of target. They often are unable to create or maintain solid friendships with their classmates. Unfortunately, it is not uncommon for passive targets to report not having a single true or close friend in their classroom environment.

Passive targets tend to be smaller and have less developed physical skills.

Passive targets also tend to be smaller and have less developed physical skills than their peers. This is particularly problematic as students begin to reach puberty, when some students develop faster than others physically. At a time when physical ability is prized by so many, students with less ability are often seen as inferior or incompetent. While small stature or less developed physical abilities do create the opportunity for teasing and other forms of harassment, they do not necessarily always result in bullying. For example, as has been indicated earlier, students who are smaller or less physically able, but who have good social skills, can develop positive friendships and are sometimes accepted as they are. They are met with good-natured humor and friendly teasing, rather than the cruelty experienced by passive targets.

These children may be targeted because of intellectual differences.

In addition to size and physical ability, intellectual abilities are also a factor in bullying. Students know who the intellectual leaders are, who is average, and who has intellectual challenges. In many schools, where there is a strong emphasis on respect for all people, students who are slower experience little interpersonal difficulty. In schools that have not established a respectful climate, the teasing and put-downs for these children can be very painful. Students with above average intellectual abilities may also experience bullying because they, too, are different.

Socioeconomic status may play a role for passive targets.

Still another area in which passive targets are vulnerable is socioeconomic status. Just as bullies can focus in on size or intellectual abilities, they are quite adept at attempting to make students with fewer financial resources feel inferior. Low-income students with good social skills and a sense of humor are often able to manage the criticisms they receive based on their family financial status with jokes or by turning the conversation in a different direction. Passive targets of bullying, though, are generally considerably less adept socially and so experience considerable pain and humiliation from their bullying peers.

Passive targets appear more anxious, nervous, and insecure than their peers.

These individuals often appear cautious and sensitive and are quiet when in social groups. These behaviors can signal that they are weak or unassertive, and they may be viewed by their peers as being unable to protect themselves or retaliate when provoked or attacked.

ACTIVITY 5.1

Reflect on your personal experiences and identify a situation you may have witnessed or directly experienced involving a passive target of bullying. Use this situation or one from this chapter to begin a discussion with your child. After sharing your experience, encourage your child to describe an incident involving a passive target.

► What happened in the incident your child describes?

_____

_____

► In addition to asking what happened, ask how your child felt and how he or she thinks the bully and target felt.

_____

_____

► Was the problem solved? If so, how? If not, how could it be solved?

_____

_____

_____

You could make this and the next two activities part of a Family Council meeting or other family time, if you wish. Other family members are likely to have much to add!

Provocative Targets

Provocative targets engage in behaviors that will actually provoke others to pick on them, tease or torment them, or engage in physical fighting. This pattern of behavior, illustrated in the following example, is much more common than many realize.

Max

Max was smaller than all of his classmates, but he was quick and energetic. He also was more immature than most of his peers, and he engaged in many childish and silly behaviors. Most of his classmates ignored or made fun of him. One of the most popular boys in class was Ray, who was well liked because of his good athletic abilities and his sense of humor. At times, he had teased Max and made fun of him.

Max began doing little things to antagonize Ray, including attempting to trip him as he walked by Max's desk, cutting in front of Ray in the lunch line, and knocking Ray's papers off his desk. Other kids saw what was happening and told Max to stop—that it wasn't funny. One day on the playground, Ray was running the bases for a long-hit ball and, as he passed third base and headed for home, Max, also on the baseball field, ran and slid under Ray's feet, causing Ray to fall and be called out. Ray was furious. When he got up, he began hitting Max and calling him names and yelling. Ray was much bigger than Max and soon had Max on the ground.

The commotion caught the eye of several teachers, who came over and hauled Ray off to the office, where he was severely chastised for fighting—particularly for beating up a much smaller boy. While the principal and several teachers had sympathy for the beating that Max got, Max's classmates had little sympathy for him and actually yelled at him for getting Ray in trouble. Max just beamed. He was so happy that he was powerful enough to get Ray, the big, popular class leader, in trouble. He got lots of attention from his classmates.

Here are some characteristics of provocative targets:

► Purposefully do things that irritate others or otherwise initiate aggression.

► Want to be seen as influential and important.

► Often strive to get other children in trouble.

► Generally, are negatively viewed by peers and school staff.

► Are at risk for serious injury if their behavior escalates.

Provocative targets purposefully do things that irritate others or otherwise initiate aggression.

Provocative targets will engage in immature acts such as making faces, mimicking and mocking, tossing things such as paper wads, and walking around knocking books off tables. While most of the examples we have discussed have been school related, the provocative target in the home is often the younger sibling—the "baby of the house" who has figured out ways to get his or her older siblings in trouble. Once older siblings react with anger and aggression, the provocative younger sibling is seen as the defenseless victim. So while passive targets of bullying basically do nothing to instigate the conflict, provocative targets have contributed to the conflict by engaging in annoying, obnoxious, and childish behaviors.

Provocative targets want to be seen as influential and important.

People frequently find it difficult to understand and empathize with provocative targets. Why would they purposefully do things that irritate others or otherwise bring aggression on themselves? Our experience in working with provocative targets suggests that they want to be seen as influential and important. Their behavior certainly helps them achieve this goal, although in a very negative way.

Provocative targets often strive to get other children in trouble.

Children who are targets often have fewer resources than their peers and enjoy getting children with greater resources in trouble. In the example, Max annoyed Ray in little ways and then pushed him over the top by tripping him on the baseball field. If the child with greater resources receives a punishment, so much the better.

Peers and school staff generally hold a negative view of provocative targets.

In the bullying experience, these are the individuals who tend to draw the least amount of sympathy from their peers—and sometimes even from their teachers. Most often, provocative targets are thought of as having "asked for it."

Are at risk for serious injury if their provocative behavior escalates.

We pay close attention to these targets because if their provocative behavior escalates, they can be seriously injured by the children they provoke. For this reason alone, it is essential for parents and teachers to take steps to help these youngsters understand their behavior and learn more adaptive ways of getting attention.

It is important to know the difference between provocative targets and children with other emotional or behavioral concerns who may engage in similar behaviors. For example, a child may hurry through the classroom and in the process knock books off other students' desks. If the child is a provocative target, we can assume he or she is attempting to get attention by engaging the other students in conflict.

The exact same behavior may occur, but if the child knocking books off desks happens to have Attention-Deficit/Hyperactivity Disorder (AD/HD), it is entirely possible that the child had no intention to disrupt or annoy others. Kids with AD/HD are often hyperactive and impulsive, and knocking books off desks is likely to be the result of their haste and completely unintended. Both the provocative target and the child with AD/HD need assistance to learn more effective ways of being around others, but they need very different interventions—a "one size fits all" approach won't work.

ACTIVITY 5.2

Share a situation involving a provocative target from your personal experience or from this chapter, then encourage your child to describe an incident of this type.

► What happened in this incident?

_____

_____

► In addition to asking what happened, ask how your child felt and how he or she thinks the bully and target felt.

_____

_____

► Was the problem solved? If so, how? If not, how could it be solved?

_____

_____

_____

Targets of Relational Bullying

The situation with Kathleen and Tanisha in chapter 4 is a good example of relational bullying. In it, Kathleen was excluded from a group of friends in retaliation for what another group member, Tanisha, perceived as an insult. Here is another one.

Laura

Sharon and Paige are two attractive girls, the best of friends, who are extremely popular at their small private school.

Their parents are well known in the community, hold prestigious jobs, and make a considerable amount of money. Due to their financially privileged status, Sharon and Paige wear the latest fashions, frequently have their hair and nails done at a trendy salon, regularly shop in the boutique specialty section of town, and dine at the nicest restaurants with their parents. Also, the two are often given lavish gifts by their families to celebrate milestones. For example, on each of the girl's recent sixteenth birthday, they received luxury automobiles, as is the custom in their parents' social group. Despite the generosity of their families, Sharon and Paige find it challenging to be kind to others. With their new cars, the nicest in the school parking lot, they have become even more brazen in their disdain for their less fortunate classmates. One of their favorite targets is Laura, "one of those scholarship students." Though Laura is intelligent, helpful, and polite, Sharon and Paige often make comments about her clothes and the fact that she is dropped off and picked up by her father in a car that is "worse than the custodian's." Prior to the winter holiday break, Laura's father was moved to a later shift, and he is no longer able to give her rides. Because of this, on many cold mornings and evenings, several of Laura's classmates see her as they pass her in their warm cars, while she waits, shivering and cold, at the public bus stop. All of the students know that to offer her a ride would bring with it the serious social consequence of exclusion.

Many people think if no one gets physically hurt, it isn't bullying—or they will agree that verbal taunting and threatening are a type of bullying. A more pervasive, insidious form of bullying is relational bullying. Relational bullying occurs when someone is systematically excluded from a group or ignored by peers. When ostracized children attempt to join the group or clique, their efforts are rejected. Although children who experience relational bullying do not experience physical harm, they do experience being ignored, treated as nonpersons, and held in contempt. Relational bullying is particularly common among girls, and it tends to increase in frequency as children get older, develop more effective verbal skills, and have a better understanding of the power of exclusion on others. Because this type of bullying isn't usually apparent to adults, it is often overlooked.

When parents wonder if relational victimization is really bullying, we ask them to apply the PIC criteria, first mentioned in chapter 1:

P—*Is it purposeful?* Relational bullying is intentional and is often well planned.

I—*Is there an imbalance of power?* Clearly, those who are doing the excluding have power over the child who is denied participation.

C—*Is it continual?* Relational bullying is rarely a single event. Once the persons doing the excluding have identified a target, they often continue to reject the individual.

Those who are able to control access to friendship and interpersonal relationships have enormous power. When they exercise this power, they show just how much the excluded child wants to be a member of the group. Revealing the excluded child's vulnerability can be very cruel.

The result of experiencing relational victimization over time is lowered self-esteem and confidence This type of bullying also may result in withdrawal, depression, anxiety, and other conditions. While the bullying itself is not physical, it affects both the physical and emotional well-being of the targeted child and warrants immediate action.

ACTIVITY 5.3

Share a situation involving a relational target from your personal experience or from this chapter, then encourage your child to describe an incident of this type.

► What happened in this incident?

_____

_____

► In addition to asking what happened, ask how your child felt and how he or she thinks the bully and target felt.

_____

_____

► Was the problem solved? If so, how? If not, how could it be solved?

_____

_____

_____

Bystanders

Vernon

Though Vernon wasn't the tallest, strongest, or brightest student in the class, he was popular. He had a sense of fair play, treated others with respect, and was generally nice to most everyone. In particular, Vernon always felt it was his responsibility to stand up for "what's right." He had a good way with words and was able to negotiate successfully; through this approach, he had gotten homework assignments shortened—one reason he was popular—and had prevented more than a few fights at lunchtime. Unfortunately, a new student had relocated to the district, and this new student was clearly aggressive. Within the first week of class, the new student had "sized everyone up" and had begun to relentlessly bully several students, calling them names and making threats. There was even a rumor that this new student had been relocated due to having gotten into too many fights at another school. Vernon quickly noticed this socially disruptive activity and decided to intervene on everyone's behalf. Vernon brought up what he had been seeing during lunchtime and tried to encourage the new student to give the aggressive behavior a rest. Unfortunately, the new student looked Vernon square in the eyes and told him that he was going to beat him up after school. The other students around him were stunned. Never had they seen Vernon's negotiation strategies fail so quickly, nor bring on such a threat of reprisal. Out of fear, no one took up Vernon's side. Instead of supporting Vernon or informing the teachers of the impending fight, the bystanders yielded to the aggression of a single student.

Many people never consider children who witness or hear about bullying incidents as being victimized by bullying behavior, but it is clear that they are also affected. Bystanders generally have one of two reactions to bullying: They are afraid that they will become the bully's next target, or they feel guilty for not coming to the aid of the child who is the target.

Many bystanders are justified in their fear that they will be targeted if they do anything to assist the target. If they take action to help, they can become the object of the bully instead of the original target. This doesn't mean that bystanders shouldn't get involved, but it does mean that they must have strength and resources or possess alternative strategies such as asking for a teacher's or parent's help.

The second response, feeling guilty for not defending the target, can have an enormous impact on bystanders. Bystander guilt often results in shame and remorse, and these emotions often can lead to sadness, depression, and general avoidance of conflict. In some cases, seeing another person being hurt or purposefully rejected but doing nothing to stop it can result in years of painful memories. Another possible outcome is "learned helplessness," a state in which children feel unable to have any impact on their own lives or the lives of others. These children frequently lose their motivation and just give up, assuming that whatever they want is out of their control. While these responses are extreme, they do happen.

It's necessary to do something about those who engage in bullying behavior and essential to provide support and safety to the direct targets of bullying. In our work with schools, we also emphasize the importance of empowering bystanders. In one school we visited, for example, an elementary school teacher was in the front of a line of children waiting to go to lunch, talking to two of the children. At the back of the line, unseen by the teacher, the last boy in line began flicking the ear of the boy in front of him. After a while, the next boy in line looked around and said to the first boy, "You're new here, so you don't know—we don't do that in our school." The offending child looked startled and said, "Oh, I didn't know" and quit flicking the other student's ear.

Students who intervene won't always be successful—at times, a bully's behavior may even escalate. However, children tend to listen to each other, and empowered bystanders are often effective in stopping aggressive behavior. If a bystander's efforts don't work, the bystander or the target can go to the teacher or another adult for help.

ACTIVITY 5.4

Share a situation in which you were a bystander in a bullying situation, or describe an example from this chapter, then encourage your child to describe a time he or she was a bystander.

► What happened in this incident?

_____

_____

► In addition to asking what happened, ask how your child felt and how he or she thinks the bully and target felt.

_____

_____

► Was the problem solved? If so, how? If not, how could it be solved?

_____

_____

_____

DIFFERENCES BETWEEN BOYS AND GIRLS

In chapter 4, we noted that although girls and boys are represented in each type of bullying behavior, they often bully in very different ways. Boys and girls also tend to experience being the target in different ways. Boys are more likely to be bullied physically than are girls and will be the target of violent or threatening behavior more often. Because it is usually physical, the bullying boys experience is generally clearly observable. Girls, on the other hand, are less likely to be physically bullied. They are more often targets of relational bullying—gossip, rumors, and social exclusion. They are also commonly bystanders, observers of physical and verbal aggression, and they experience the fear and guilt associated with such bullying.

SUMMARY AND CONCLUSIONS

In this chapter, we described four types of target: passive, provocative, relational, and bystander. Because it is subtle, people sometimes don't realize the impact relational bullying, with its rumors and social exclusion, has on targets. Another group not commonly thought of as victimized is bystanders, although they clearly experience fear and guilt when they witness or hear about bullying incidents. The next two chapters describe a number of ways to help bullies and targets, including bystanders.

CHAPTER 6

Helping Children Who Bully

If you have been reading this book straight through from the beginning, you've covered quite a bit of territory! Chapter 1 gave a definition of bullying and several examples of what is and isn't considered bullying. It also attempted to dispel some myths about bullying that teachers and parents commonly hold. In chapter 2, we talked about risk and protective factors associated with bullying and discussed what is in parents' sphere of influence to change and what resources parents can consult for assistance. Chapter 3 focused on tools families we've worked with have found helpful. Chapters 4 and 5 pointed out the characteristics of different types of bullies and targets.

In this chapter, we'll take a look at ways to help children who bully. We'll discuss the importance of giving these children opportunities to learn skills that will help them choose positive behaviors instead of bullying. The skill areas most important for children who bully include anger and impulse control, cognitive retraining, empathy, and problem solving. Before reading about these areas, however, consider the following warning signs for bullying and general suggestions for what to do to intervene.

Ten Warning Signs for Bullying

1. Frequent initiation of fights
2. Disrespect toward authority figures
3. Lack of concern about whether other people's feelings are hurt or even apparent pleasure from hurting others
4. Unwillingness to acknowledge mistakes or take responsibility for mistakes
5. Disregard for rules
6. Lack of fear
7. Teasing or intentionally harming pets or other animals
8. Lying in order to get out of trouble or avoid negative consequences
9. Use of anger and aggression to get one's own way
10. Unwillingness to trust or open up to other people

Think about the behavior of your child or of another child you know. Circle the numbers of the items describing the child's behavior. If the child engages in some or most of these behaviors in different settings—school, home, community—and with a number of different people, it is likely that he or she has an aggressive, bullying style of social interaction.

Discuss your responses with your parenting partner or other parents, if you wish. If your child has many of these warning signs, also discuss the following recommendations and plan ways to make changes accordingly.

What You Can Do

Remember the discussion of modeling from chapter 3? Briefly, modeling means that children observe and model their behavior after the behavior they see, especially their parents' behavior. If your children observe you or other adults bullying, being aggressive, showing disrespect, or humiliating others, you can be certain the behavior won't go unnoticed and will likely show up at school or in the community. It's important to model the kind of behavior you want your child to use.

If the following kinds of measures and any plans that have been set up with the school do not result in noticeable changes in your child's behavior, then you should get in touch with a mental health professional for more help.

Signal your disapproval of bullying.

Many parents assume that their children will know they disapprove of this behavior, but when parents laugh at examples of bullying in cartoons, movies, or television—or worse yet, in real life—their children often assume that while their parents might say they don't like bullying, in fact they do, and they even find it funny.

Also signal your refusal to tolerate bullying in any form.

Bullying is a major problem, a serious issue, and parents must inform their children that they will not tolerate it, condone it, or pretend it isn't happening. They must then follow through to demonstrate their commitment to stopping the problem. This involves "catching children being good" and letting them know how much you value and appreciate their behaving as they do. It also means not letting bullying or aggressive behaviors slip by but instead providing an immediate consequence each and every time for bullying behavior. While this will require a time commitment early in the process, children very quickly get the message.

Say what you mean and mean what you say.

Many parents fail to have rules they will actually enforce or family expectations they hold for all members. For example, to say "I'm warning you" when a child already knows he or she is engaging in unacceptable behavior does not convey that you mean what you say; rather, the child learns it is possible to get away with several infractions of the rule before there will be a consequence. If you intend for your child to stop doing something immediately, say it with meaning and then follow through with a consequence if he or she violates the rule even once. We have learned over and over in our family groups and in working with students in detention centers and juvenile court settings how much they value parents' setting reasonable limits and then holding them accountable. Consequences should "fit the crime"—that is, it isn't reasonable to have an extraordinary punishment for a small infraction—but it is important that there be a timely (right away) and reasonable (fair) consequence. A time-out, loss of allowance, or restriction on some other privilege, such as locking up the Game Boy, iPod, or bicycle, is likely to have quite an impact.

Develop your family environment so that people want to be in one another's company.

One way to accomplish this is to have family time every day, providing an opportunity for each person to relate to others in the family through talk, games, and other connecting activities. Children who feel prized and valued by their families develop self-confidence and self-esteem as well as interpersonal skills that help them get along with others without ever having to resort to force, coercion, or bullying.

Support your children's interests.

All children like to feel influential. Facilitating their participation in sports and other activities that require them to interact positively, play by the rules, and learn to be a team player can have a significant impact.

SKILLS FOR CHILDREN WHO BULLY

Children of all ages are actively engaged in acquiring certain developmental skills, or skills relating to thinking, feeling, and behaving that are expected at a particular level of development. Many children appear to master these skills without special effort. We know, however, that a significant minority of children don't acquire these skills automatically. That's the bad news. The good news is that most of these skills can be taught. As parents, we have a great deal of influence over our children's acquisition of these skills.

Your child's school also may have a program designed to teach specific social skills, either in small groups or the classroom. If so, instruction generally involves a four-step process, in which a teacher or trainer (1) models the skill for students to observe, (2) conducts a role-playing exercise in which students enact the skill, (3) encourages group observers to give feedback on how well the skill was enacted and what might make it better, and (4) gives students a "homework assignment" to practice the skill in the real world. These are the very same steps you can use in your home to help your child acquire social skills. An example of this four-step process appears in chapter 7, on helping targets, in which a parent helps her child make friends by teaching her child the skill of joining in a group.

As you will soon see, anger and impulse control, cognitive retraining, empathy, and problem-solving strategies are among the most important skills for children who bully.

Anger and Impulse Control

Children and adolescents who bully are commonly both aggressive and impulsive. When these children feel an emotion strongly, they tend to respond immediately, without thinking through the consequences of their behavior. Children experience impulsivity in three ways: intellectually, emotionally, and physically. Children who experience their impulses intellectually tend to think about what it is that they desire with increasing focus and intensity. They often may be aware of these thought patterns as they are occurring; however, they frequently have difficulty recognizing that these thought patterns eventually result in impulsive behaviors. For example, a child may be jealous of another child who brought a new game in for show-and-tell. The first child fixates on the game, thinking about how much fun it would be to own, play with, and use as a means of gaining respect from her peers. She may have pictures in her mind about what these things would look like, or she may think the thoughts in words. Either way, each thought fuels the next.

Children who have emotional experiences that lead to impulse control problems tend to have a lot of their behavior driven by their mood states. For example, a child may be particularly excited or sad or angry and become so overwhelmed with these emotions that he may lose sight of his ability to think about the consequences of certain actions. Or a child who feels sad because he is experiencing social isolation may bully another child to gain attention from his peers or adults. For example, a child may be having what his parents call a "blue day." Ever since waking up, he is pouty and negative, sensitive and irritable. His parents worry after putting him on the bus in the morning, for they know there is a high likelihood that he will snap at a peer or teacher and come home with a report of negative behavior. As they predict, during lunch he disregards a teacher's instruction that he sit down and is sent to the principal's office.

Children who experience impulse control physically might feel tension in their bodies or have tingling or dizziness, headaches, or stomachaches. For these children, bodily sensations are the most significant way in which they experience their world. A child who experiences impulsivity physically might describe the events that led up to an aggressive behavior as being like electricity she felt in her body. For example, a student may be sitting in the back of her middle school prealgebra class, bored and wishing for lunch. All of a sudden, she feels the hair on her arms and neck stand on end, and she becomes pleasantly energized. She becomes fidgety and talkative, then blurts out an insulting comment about another student without thinking.

Teaching children to recognize their "triggers"—the events and settings that usually lead to their impulsive actions—will help them recognize times they are in a situation that could lead to bullying behavior. Such triggers may be external (for example, being pushed or called a name) or internal (for example, feeling ice in the veins or a racing heart). Consider the girl who is fixated on a toy another child brought in for show-and-tell: Her parents could ask her to imagine getting a similar toy at the end of the week or marking period as a reward for having good behavior. They could help her learn how to shift her thoughts to imagine herself getting positive attention (and a gift) from proud and happy, accepting family members.

The parents of the boy having a "blue day" could encourage him to recognize the power that his mood states have and help him to work on changing his feelings from sad to happy by focusing on remembering what it feels like to be happy and in a good mood, perhaps by recalling a funny movie or joke.

The parents of the girl who was distracted from math by the "electricity" moving across her body might suggest that she try discreetly to alternate flexing and relaxing her thighs or biceps while sitting relatively still in her chair. Or she could rub her arms and thighs, as if she were cold and trying to warm herself up. These activities would give her something else to think about and, since it is difficult for the mind to focus on two sensations with equal amounts of attention, act as a sort of "circuit breaker."

The next time your child has difficulty controlling impulsive behavior, in addition to asking what happened, find out whether your child experienced any triggers in the moments immediately before the incident. Ask the following questions:

▶ What happened?

_____

_____

_____

▶ What were you thinking and feeling before you lost control?

_____

_____

_____

If your child is able to identify a trigger, give praise for self-awareness. If your child is unable to identify any triggering thoughts, feelings, or sensations, encourage him or her to pay attention to these experiences in the future.

To help your child think of more positive ways to cope with similar situations, you can also ask this question:

▶ What could you do if you have these thoughts and feelings again instead of losing control?

_____

_____

Being able to identify triggers is an important first step in coping with these types of challenges. Continue to ask about triggers and the situations in which your child experiences them.

Remember, as a parent your role is to help your child learn and grow, whether that involves tying shoes, understanding fractions, or becoming more self-aware. If a child can learn to identify thoughts, feelings, and sensations that serve as triggers, he or she can begin to recognize them as friends rather than foes and use them on the path toward developing better behavioral control.

Cognitive Retraining: A New Way of Thinking

Children who are not generally aggressive tend to interpret a bump, shove, or tactless comment by a peer as no big deal. Children who bully, on the other hand, tend to believe that these actions are malicious and that they must retaliate—even when it is clear to objective observers that the action was not meant to harm. Aggressive children can benefit from learning to think in a different way. (Researchers and mental health workers call this *cognitive retraining*.) Activities that include taking another's perspective or doing role-reversals can help children who are quick to blame others learn that alternate ways of thinking exist.

Joanne

Joanne came home one night with a behavior report for bullying another girl in her social studies class. When her father asked her to explain, Joanne said that the reason she wanted to fight the other girl was that the girl kept passing notes to other students saying bad things about Joanne. Joanne's father asked a few questions and quickly came to realize that Joanne didn't know what the notes contained. Realizing that Joanne was misreading the situation, he decided to use the "talking out loud" technique to encourage Joanne to come up with as many thoughts as she could that the other girl might be having about her. They made it a silly game and took turns generating both funny and serious, plausible and implausible, things the girl might be writing in the notes. Some of the things were mean, some were nice, some were jealous, and, toward the end of the game, most weren't even about Joanne at all—they were about the boring coursework. The next time Joanne saw the girl pass a note in class, she was reminded of her talk with her father. She didn't experience the sudden flash of suspiciousness and anger—she just smiled and got back to her work.

As we all know, thinking is a private process. As adults, we often understand that everyone thinks a little bit differently; this is why no two people describe the same auto accident the same way. Children, however, need to develop this understanding, and, of course, some develop it more quickly than others.

ACTIVITY 6.3

If your child tends to misattribute aggressive motives to others, the next time you see this happening we suggest that you stop the child and think through the situation together. Try asking these questions:

► What happened?

_____

_____

_____

► Why do you think the person did that?

_____

_____

► What are some other reasons the person might have done that?

_____

_____

_____

Help your child identify as many motives as possible for what happened. Make it a game: Praise your child for generating ideas, regardless of how implausible they might be.

Feel free to add your own ideas to illustrate a nondefensive way to perceive the experience. "Prime the pump" by showing the individuals involved in the situation in a neutral or even positive light.

Empathy

Empathy is the ability to understand what someone else is thinking and feeling—and the ability to communicate that awareness. Ideally, children learn through early experiences in their families and neighborhoods to understand and care about other people. As we know, however, not all children have or benefit equally from these early childhood experiences. For these children, exposure to other children and adults who model appropriate empathic behaviors can be helpful. As you might imagine, building empathy is crucial for children who bully. If children who bully become more aware of the emotional (and perhaps physical) toll they are taking on their victims, they are less likely to be inclined to continue their aggressive behavior. Empathy is also crucial to a key component in the development of mature moral judgment, which involves an understanding of the need to treat others with respect and dignity.

As a parent, you are in a perfect position to model empathic behaviors for your child. You can encourage empathy by watching a movie or television program with your child and asking your child to tell you what different characters are thinking and feeling (see Activity 3.4, on page 46). By doing this activity, you encourage your child to step into the experience of other people.

ACTIVITY 6.4

Encourage empathy in real-life situations as they arise by continuing to ask your child these questions:

► What do you think _____ is thinking?

► What is _____ feeling?

► How would you feel if this happened to you?

Problem Solving

In the same way that children learn impulse control and empathy through observation, they learn to solve problems through interactions with other children and adults. Children who bully often don't know how to get what they want and need in an appropriate manner. If children who bully are able to recognize that healthier, more effective ways of interacting with others are possible, they will be less likely to engage in bullying behaviors in the future.

The Big Questions, introduced in chapter 3, are a simple problem-solving process that you can employ to show your child an alternative way of approaching a difficult situation. In chapter 3, we saw how one parent used the Big Questions: Theresa's son Lee had been getting into behavioral conflicts at school and was bringing home notes from the teacher and counselor about the misbehavior. Theresa was quite distraught and yelled at Lee, and she even threatened to hurt him if the behavior didn't stop. Lee yelled back at Theresa, then slammed and locked his door. After settling down, Theresa reviewed the Big Questions, which Lee's school counselor had given her. She decided that the steps she had been taking were not working and that she needed to try something different. She made a list of other steps she could take, including spending more time with Lee when she was calm, talking with him about what was happening in school that led to such conflicts, and spending time with the counselor attempting to learn more effective ways of managing Lee's behavior.

Here's a second example, showing how another parent used this approach in a situation involving relational bullying.

Patty and Mary

Mary found out that her daughter, Patty, had been intentionally embarrassing one of her classmates. Patty had been repeatedly telling another girl that she was not invited to Patty's sleepover this coming Friday. When Patty's teacher called Mary to express her concern over how disruptive Patty's gloating had become, Mary decided to try to intervene. Using the Big Questions, she determined that her goal was to provide Patty with an incentive to stop bullying her classmate. Mary realized that she had authorized the sleepover, even though Patty had been having occasional behavioral problems at school and that most of the problems related to this sort of exclusionary behavior. Mary decided that she might be unintentionally reinforcing this unwanted behavior since she rarely provided Patty with negative consequences that amounted to more than a "talking to." Since talking had proven to be ineffective, she decided to restrict Patty's privilege of having the sleepover and to tell Patty exactly why she was no longer allowed to have her friends over. In addition, Mary decided that she would allow Patty to earn back this privilege if she could go to school for two weeks with no behavioral problems. Though Mary knew that it would likely be a chaotic evening when she told Patty of the change and new expectations, she knew in her heart that effective parenting involves praise and punishment, support and challenge. By the next marking period, Patty had significantly fewer behavior problems at school and home.

The STOPP procedure is another problem-solving strategy. You can use this one instead of the Big Questions if it is easier to remember.

S—*Stop:* Stop, settle down, and be calm.

T—*Think:* Think about the problem and your goals.

O—*Options:* Think about the options or solutions to the problem.

P—*Plan:* Examine the consequences of different options, choose the best, and do it.

P—*Plan working?* If it is, congratulations. This is a signal to continue. If it isn't, consider what you could do differently to cause the plan to work better or select another plan to carry out.

ACTIVITY 6.5

Discuss a problem your child has or has had. (The problem may or may not be related to bullying.) Describe it here:

_____

_____

_____

Work through the Big Questions together, using the Big Questions Form (see Figure 9, on page 44) to record your child's responses, if you wish.

1. What is your goal?
2. What are you doing?
3. Is what you are doing helping you achieve your goal?
4. If not, what can you do differently?

Remember to ask the Big Questions in a supportive way, with the goal of finding a more effective solution to the problem, not as a way to punish the child.

This activity could also be the subject of a Family Council meeting or other family time.

SUMMARY AND CONCLUSIONS

After giving the warning signs of bullying and some possible responses parents can make, we pointed out that children who bully lack skills in certain areas, especially as concerns anger and impulse control, thinking objectively, empathy, and problem solving. Fortunately, these skills can be taught, both formally, in the school, and informally, in day-to-day life. You can help your child recognize what kinds of people and situations trigger his or her anger, question your child's thinking about whether events happen on purpose or accidentally, ask your child to consider how others feel, and use the Big Questions to help your child solve problems in a way that doesn't hurt others. All of these strategies can help reduce a child's aggression; the next chapter focuses on helping targets of children who bully.

CHAPTER
7
Helping Targets of Bullying

Chapter 6 concerned ways parents can help children who bully. This chapter focuses on targets of bullying. In it, we look at skill areas important in helping children avoid and respond effectively to bullying—particularly as they relate to friendships, assertive communication, and asking for help. Bystanders are targets, too, and they have specific concerns related to their role in the bullying situation. Before we move on to discuss these topics, however, please consider the following list of warning signs for this group and steps for reducing the likelihood that your child will become a target.

Ten Warning Signs for Targets of Bullying

1. Physical signs of fighting, such as bruises, scratches, or bite marks; torn or missing clothing

2. Frequent illnesses or trouble sleeping

3. Sudden decrease in school performance

4. Peer rejection

5. Depression, unexplained or uncontrolled crying, thoughts or talk of suicide

6. Avoiding certain groups at school, unwillingness to walk to or from school

7. Sudden and unexplained changes in request for certain lunch items

8. Development of tics, nail biting or hair pulling, or bed-wetting or soiling (in younger children)

9. Truancy or refusing to go to school or attend other activities

10. Avoiding previously enjoyable activities (for instance, recess or lunchtime; going to neighborhood gatherings)

Think about the behavior of your child or of another child you know. Circle the numbers of the items describing the child's behavior. If the child engages in some or most of these behaviors in different settings—school, home, community—and with a number of different people, it is it is possible that he or she may be the target of bullying.

Discuss your responses with your parenting partner or other parents, if you wish. If your child has many of these warning signs, also discuss the following recommendations and plan ways to make changes accordingly.

What You Can Do

There are a number of steps parents can take to help reduce the likelihood that their children will become the targets of bullying. Some that we often share with parents include the following.

Prize your child.

Life can be difficult, and many children experience considerable hassles and sometimes even abuse in their daily lives. The family should be a place where every child knows he or she is important, valued, and loved. While this does not mean overlooking problems, it does mean making sure that even when corrections are needed, they are delivered in a loving and respectful manner so the child knows he or she is prized, even with blemishes in the behavior. Here's how one dad did just that:

> Jamal, I understand that you got into a hassle with Joseph at school today and that he and several others were picking on you. I can see how you would lose your temper after a little of that and want to shut them up, but we can't have you doing it the way you did—hitting Joseph is not acceptable. You know I love you and want what's best for you, and having you get into trouble with Joseph and having the school come down on your case isn't in your best interest. Let's talk about how we can handle this situation differently if it comes up again.

Praise your child.

Much of our society is based on competition and negative comparisons. If you doubt that, consider reality television shows and competitive sports, in which winning is all. Children sometimes go through whole days without any positive affirmation of who they are. Families should be affirming and supportive, and parents need to spend time "catching their children being good" so they can give lots of positive feedback. We recommend a formula of at least three positives for every negative, even if it means hunting for opportunities to be encouraging and positive.

ACTIVITY 7.2

We call this activity for the whole family "Did You Notice?"

► Explain to your family that each member will decide in the morning to do at least one good deed for each other person in the family during the day.

► At the end of the day, bring the family together to guess what good things each person did.

When the guessing begins, each person guesses several things—thus demonstrating that every person in the family does good things and that everyone is deserving of recognition and praise for doing them.

Promote humor and good times.

The old expression "laughter is the best medicine" is often true. Many families focus so much on the negative and difficult times they experience that they have little time for fun and laughter, yet those are events that bring the family together, promote family cohesion, and create memories worth remembering. This means finding fun things to do and ways of approaching life with good humor rather than negativism. It means avoiding cruel teasing, mean jokes, or harassing family members over things they can't control (needing glasses, having red hair, etc.). It also means helping children learn how to identify jokes that are funny but not harmful to other people (like the cute poem about pelicans: "What a strange bird is the pelican/Its bill can hold more than its belly can").

Try telling funny stories, thinking of riddles and puzzles, playing the game "Are You Smarter Than a Fifth Grader?" watching funny videos about people or animals, or buying a joke book to take turns reading aloud.

Problem-solve instead of punish.

Punishment is usually undertaken for the satisfaction of the person who feels as if he or she has been wronged. When a parent begins focusing on punishment, it's time to stop and go through the Big Questions (What's my goal? What am I doing? Is it working? What could I do differently?) and determine whether the punishment is designed to solve a problem or to wreak vengeance. The goal of effective parenting is to create responsible children, and engaging them in problem solving is usually much more effective than focusing on punishment (though discipline in the form of losing a privilege or opportunity can be part of problem solving). Here's how one mom approached a tricky bullying situation with her daughter:

> We've got a problem, Marta. You've been picked on by other kids at school, and I understand that. But you cannot be in fights at school, nor can you come home and act rude to your family because someone offended you at school. Let's talk about what we can do to manage this problem better. We can begin by the two us going to the counselor and talking about steps to be taken at school. But we also have to have an agreement that your behavior at home will be responsible and not obnoxious. If you are responsible, we'll have good times together and enjoy one another's company, but if you come in obnoxious like you did today, there has to be a consequence because we aren't your enemies—we are your family, we love you, and we won't tolerate this behavior. Let's talk about what a reasonable consequence may be if you act like this again, and let's talk about steps we can take to help you make sure you'll remember to behave more appropriately so we don't have to put any consequences into action.

Practice what you preach.

Many parents have no idea of the extent to which their children admire them and see them as models of how to live life. (Kids are unlikely to tell their parents this because it would be a betrayal of kid culture!) We continue interviewing elementary, middle, and high school students regularly, inquiring about how they learn how to behave (all the way from getting along in first grade to managing advances on a blind date). Their most consistent answer? Parents. Even when the parents haven't had specific discussions about how they should conduct themselves, children explain that they see how their parents live their lives and draw conclusions from their observations. They also listen to how their parents talk, what they say as they watch television or movies, and the comments they make to friends—and they see how their parents treat strangers. Telling a child one thing and then behaving in a way inconsistent with that not only teaches the children what to do (as compared to what to say), it also teaches them dishonesty. We can't always be perfect, but when we do make mistakes and our children see them, it is perfectly legitimate to have a talk about being a fallible human being who makes mistakes but then tries to correct them rather than lie about them or deny that they happened. Here's how one dad's admission that he overreacted modeled an appropriate way to respond to making a mistake:

> I would like to talk to you about how I handled myself last night, Kima. When I found out about your poor math grade, I overreacted. First, I want you to know that I love you and want you to be successful, and that means I get concerned about your grades when they don't reflect your potential. Second, I want you to know that I make mistakes, too, and don't always live up to my potential. My overreaction was an example of this. I wish that I had been calmer and hadn't yelled and said some of the things I said. I still think that your video games and TV watching are distracting you from your studies; however, I don't think it is fair or realistic to take both of them away for a month. Staring tomorrow, you can pick either the television or your game system and have it for 30 minutes—after you have shown me your completed home-work. Again, I want to apologize for overreacting last night. It's okay to fail from time to time, as long as we recognize it, admit it, and make attempts to change it.

Preserve your promises.

If your child is being teased, taunted, or mistreated in some way at school or in the neighborhood and you say you will take steps to help alleviate the problem, then follow through. This is true whether the promise was in relation to a bullying problem or anything else—children expect their parents to keep their word, to follow through on promises, and to honor agreements. While on occasion there are exceptions (you can't go to the park during a hurricane; you can't go to a school function with the flu; you can't go because of work), children learn how important they are by how reliably their parents keep agreements and meet obligations. Children need to be able to rely upon their parents, above all others.

To stay in touch with the school, schedule a meeting or phone conference with your child's teacher or counselor. Let your child know that you are planning to do this. Ask your child to tell you about any concerns and how he or she would like you to address them (if you are really creative, use the Big Questions in a Family Council meeting so everyone can see how invested you are in supporting family members). Then take notes—mentally or on paper—so when you have the meeting, you can be sure to address all of the concerns. After the meeting, discuss any developments and work with your child and other family members, if appropriate, to chart a new direction.

Promote consistency.

Children have an uncanny knack for testing the limits to see what they can get away with. They will often have tantrums, create conflict, or become stubborn to see what their parents will do. Many parents give in to their children's coercion—they find it easier to let the child have his or her way than to engage in conflict. Conflict is an excellent teaching tool for children: It teaches parents to give in, to lack consistency, to avoid responsible parenting . . . all of which are mistakes. In our work in elementary through high schools, children and adolescents consistently tell us that they want their parents to set reasonable limits and hold to them. Among other things, firm limits provide kids with an excuse to engage in responsible behavior: "Oh, I'd like to do that, but my parents would kill me . . ."

Preston

> Preston went to a neighborhood party, where, it turned out, no parents were home to chaperone. There was drinking, even though several of the kids felt uncomfortable with it. Chuck, one of the local tough kids, yelled at Preston, "When I drink, everyone drinks!" Several looked at Preston to see what he would do. Preston smiled and said, "Chuck, I understand you, man, but you don't have to go home to my momma . . . Now, if you want to walk up the street and ask her about me drinking, I'll wait here for you, at least until I hear the ambulance coming." At that, the other kids broke out laughing, and Chuck said, "I've met your momma, and I'm not messing with her." After that, he left Preston alone.

ADVICE FOR TARGETS

Targets of bullying frequently get bad advice from adults who hang on to myths about bullying. They are often advised to ignore their tormentors or walk away; however, ignoring bullying without adult support is unlikely to be successful. Standing up to the bully, also a common suggestion, is equally unlikely to change the situation and actually may make a bad situation worse. Some adults advise targets to fight back. However, retaliation with name-calling or physical aggression just creates more tension in the relationship and makes the struggle more public—something the bully may actually desire.

Acting helpless or submitting to the bully is not likely to result in any improvement either. In fact, acting helpless is probably the behavior that attracted the bully in the first place. Children who bully choose targets they perceive as weak, so it is important to help targets build upon their strengths. Although targets have no control over certain characteristics (for instance, height or race), they can exercise control over some of the behaviors that tend to draw bullies to them. For example, the more intensely targets react to bullies, the more likely the bullying behavior is to continue. When targets reduce the intensity of their reactions, they rob bullies of their emotional payoffs.

Children who bully come to expect their targets to respond in certain ways. So if targets can choose unexpected, "nonvictim" responses, they may be able to reduce the likelihood that the bullying will continue. The following example shows how.

Jonathan

Every time Gabriel engages in bullying behaviors toward Jonathan, Jonathan responds by trying to make himself invisible, moving toward a corner of the room and trembling in fear. Gabriel enjoys this predictable response from Jonathan and knows that Jonathan will always meet his emotional needs because he responds in the same way every time! But, since practicing his nonvictim responses with his dad each evening, Jonathan has decided to try a different response the next time Gabriel bullies him. Jonathan has decided not to retreat to a corner of the room. Instead, as he sees Gabriel coming, he walks toward him, saying, "What can I help you with today?" Then he continues walking toward the front of the class, where the teacher's desk is located. Gabriel is so confused by this new behavior that he doesn't know what to do!

The suggestion that children who are targeted change their behavior is in no way intended to suggest that children who are targeted for aggression are responsible for their own pain. It is easy to fall into the trap of "blaming the victim." We can't stress strongly enough that *targets need adult support and protection to stop the aggression immediately.*

SKILLS FOR TARGETS

Children who bully are not the only ones who can benefit from instruction in the skills needed to interact effectively with others. Targets of bullying often lack the skills needed to communicate and deal with conflicts. Research and our personal experiences with families help us to say, with confidence, that teaching such skills helps children cope more effectively with bullying. Schools sometimes offer programs designed to teach specific social skills for both children who bully and their targets. Generally, a teacher or trainer models the skill for students to observe, conducts a role-playing exercise using the skill, encourages group observers to give feedback on how well the skill was performed, and gives students the assignment to practice the skill in the real world. For targets, skills relating to friendships, assertive communication, and help seeking are especially important.

The Importance of Friendships

Friendships are vitally important to children of all ages. Having friends tends to insulate children from bullying and, when they are bullied, helps them cope with it. Unfortunately, many targets of bullying are children with few friends. Although there are many reasons for this, two common reasons warrant in-depth exploration—children's expectations for their interactions with other children and their knowledge of and ability to use friendship skills.

Targets of bullying often have low self-esteem, sometimes based on their having less developed social and physical skills than their peers. Unfortunately, these children's self-perceptions of their social competence (whether accurate or not) can lead them to feel anxious and awkward. Their tendency to feel this way can actually create a self-fulfilling prophecy of social rejection: They expect other children to reject them, approach other children in a way that can lead to rejection, and then go away having their initial expectations confirmed. Over time, a series of these expectations of failure and rejection lead to increased feelings of anxiety, eventually causing these children to dread and avoid almost all social interactions.

As adults, we expect occasional social failures, but we recognize that we will have successes, too. Sometimes children have trouble making this leap of faith. You can help your child overcome this cycle of negative expectations by becoming your child's "social coach." A good social coach helps a child identify negative thoughts and feelings about a situation and then gently and honestly encourages the child to form more positive thoughts and expectations.

You can also use the social-coaching approach to encourage your child to learn and use specific skills for making and keeping friends. To help your child develop a more confident and self-assured manner, for example, you could break the friendship-making skill of joining a group down into these steps:

1. Stand up straight.
2. Walk tall.

3. Make direct eye contact.

4. Ask if you can join the group.

The following example shows how one child's mother and brother helped her practice these steps in real life.

Sophie

Sophie had been at a new school for the last two months, but she continued to sit alone during lunch. She was always close to other groups of students but was never quite part of the conversation. Sometimes Sophie heard other kids talking about her and about how weird they thought it was that she didn't talk to anyone. Sophie wanted to make new friends, but she just didn't know how to walk up to a group of strangers and start talking. Sophie's mom and older brother helped her figure out what steps she could use to approach the group. Next, they pretended they were having a conversation about plans for an upcoming school event, and Sophie practiced the steps. Her mom told her that using the steps might or might not work, and that if they didn't work, Sophie might feel a little sad or embarrassed, but she could try again with another group. The next day, Sophie tried out her new skill. She stood up straight and walked over to three girls from her class who were sitting down at lunch and talking. She made eye contact with one of the girls and asked if she could join the conversation. Sophie was happy to find that the girls asked her to sit down with them.

The goal of social coaching is twofold—first, to help the child identify and practice effective friendship skills and, second, to help the child become more comfortable about the experience of being with others. With practice, children can learn to change how they think of themselves socially. As they begin to experience themselves as being more effective socially, others will as well!

Assertive Communication

Learning to communicate in an appropriately assertive way is important for *all* children, but it is especially helpful for children who are frequent targets of aggression. Being assertive means standing up for your rights by expressing your feelings and desires in a direct way, while respecting the rights of others. There is a big difference between being assertive and being aggressive. Aggression involves getting what you want by violating the rights of others—for example, by physical force or threats. This style of interaction is the bully's stock in trade. In contrast, children who do not know how to ask for what they want and need often adopt a passive style of interaction that rarely gives them the opportunity to say what *they* want. Table 3 shows how these communication styles differ. If a child is targeted and does not know how to be appropriately assertive, he or she is likely to hold in negative emotions, something that may damage that child's self-esteem and well-being or cause the child to "blow up" when the abuse becomes too much.

Learning to use "I-messages" instead of "you-messages" is a specific way to help children express their feelings and wishes assertively. It is common for kids—and adults—to use you-messages when they feel threatened or angry. You-messages put the other person on the defensive because they assign blame. I-messages, on the other hand, are an honest and respectful way to let someone else know how their behavior is affecting you. The examples in Table 4 illustrate the difference.

ACTIVITY 7.3

Practice using I-messages with your child. Provide examples from your own experience, if possible. For example, instead of demanding that your boss give you a raise (aggressive) or simply not asking (passive), you could describe an assertive way of asking for one:

> The cost of living keeps going up, and I haven't had a salary increase in more than a year. At the same time, I've been increasing my skills by learning the new computer program. I need a salary increase and believe it is deserved; I'd appreciate your considering that seriously.

▶ When are some times you could use I-messages with your child?

_____

_____

_____

▶ When are some times your child could use I-messages with you or others?

_____

_____

_____

Look for opportunities to use I-messages instead of you-messages, and ask other members of your family to do the same. Practice using I-messages whenever opportunities arise and provide lots of encouragement and support for using them.

Table 3 Passive, Assertive, and Aggressive Responses

Passive	Assertive	Aggressive
"Okay, here's my money."	"I'm using my money for my lunch."	"I'm telling everyone you're a thief."
Does nothing when teased.	"Please stop teasing me—it isn't funny."	Hits the teaser.
Picks up books when they are knocked to the floor.	"Please don't do that—it's an unnecessary way to get attention."	Goes to the bully's desk and knocks books off his or her desk.
Ignores being inappropriately touched in the hallway.	"Inappropriate touching is sexual harassment, which is against the law. Stop it now."	Slaps the offender.
Cries when shoved in the hall.	"Please stop" (and follow up action with an adult if necessary).	Runs and hits the offender in the back of the head.

Table 4 You-Messages versus I-Messages

You-messages	I-messages
"You're such a jerk!"	"When you tease like that, I feel irritated because it is so unnecessary; please stop now."
"You make me so mad!"	"When you call me names, I get upset and angry, and that doesn't help anything. I'd like you to stop calling me names. If you've got a problem with me, let me know what it is so we can talk about it."
"You're always doing such stupid things."	"I know you're just trying to be cute, but when you do these silly things it embarrasses me, and I wish you wouldn't do them. Surely there's some other way we can spend time together."

Asking for Help

As adults, we know help seeking is very important. For example, for health treatment, we seek advice and guidance from doctors. For tax services, we seek help from tax preparers and accountants. For conflicts in the family, we seek family counseling or guidance from a religious leader or trained therapist. Help seeking demonstrates a healthy approach to managing problems that are beyond our control, and it is essential for children to learn that seeking help is legitimate, acceptable, and even expected when it is appropriate to do so.

We sometimes take for granted that children who are bullied will come to us for help if they need it. We wish this were the case, but not all children know how. All children should learn the steps in asking for help:

1. Decide what the problem is.

   Who or what is causing the problem? How do you feel when the problem happens?

2. Do you want help with the problem?

   Sometimes we can solve problems by ourselves. Is this a problem you have been able to solve by yourself in the past, or is this a problem you need help with?

3. Who can help you?

   Name as many people as you can who would listen and help (for example, the school counselor, another teacher, a classmate, a peer).

4. Ask a person if you can talk to him or her about the problem, tell the person the problem, and talk about ways you can solve the problem together.

   You may decide that you need someone else's help as well.

Some children know how to ask for help—but they simply don't do it. Unfortunately, many children ask adults for help with a bullying problem but don't receive it. As a result, they figure that it's pointless to expect assistance and assume that they are in it alone. Other children may be embarrassed to admit that they are targets of bullying or afraid that if they seek help, the bullying will just get worse. Here's how one mother helped her daughter figure out a way to ask for help when she needed it.

Sally

Sally has been getting picked on a lot on the bus. In particular, Jean has been calling her names and throwing things at her. Understandably, Sally is very upset by this, and she has started feeling nervous and sad every time she needs to get on the bus. Following an especially difficult ride home, Sally told her mother about the troubles she has been having. First, Sally's mom comforted her by letting her know that she is a wonderful child and that it wasn't anything Sally did that caused this: Sally is a kind and lovable child. Second, Sally's mom reassured her and let her know that she would call the school and set up an appointment with the principal and counselor to make them aware of the situation (when one child is bullied, everyone is at risk). Third, Sally's mom talked to Sally about asking for help.

With her mother's assistance, Sally was first able to understand that being bullied is not okay and that it is her right to ride the bus without being tormented. When her mother asked her about needing help, Sally said she thought she would need support in stopping the bullying—Jean was just "too big" and "too mean." Sally and her mother identified the bus driver as someone who might be able to help when the bullying started. Sally's mother decided to call the school and set up a meeting with the counselor and bus driver so Sally would be able to become comfortable with the bus driver in a no-stress situation. In the meeting, Sally decided she would sit toward the front of the bus so she could ask the driver for help if she needed it.

ACTIVITY 7.4

Does your child know when and how to ask for help if a bullying situation arises?

► Ask your child if he or she knows how to ask for help.

► Teach the steps in help seeking, if necessary.

► Identify by name adults in the school and community that your child could go to for help.

► Encourage your child to tell you right away about any bullying that occurs.

Follow up on your child's use of this skill and be sure to provide lots of support.

HELP FOR BYSTANDERS

The most promising group of new friends consists of children who are currently bystanders, many of whom would be willing to provide support by spending time with targets, inviting them to get involved in group activities, encouraging their efforts and accomplishments, and just being good listeners.

Bystanders are a potential source of help to targets, but they are also targets themselves. Who are bystander targets? They are the vast majority of children in a school who are not directly involved in the situation but who witness or are exposed to it indirectly (by hearing about the event from others, for example). Many people don't consider bystanders in bullying situations to be targets, but clearly, they are also negatively affected.

Bystander Reactions

Bystanders generally have one of two reactions to witnessing a bullying situation: fear or guilt. Many bystanders are afraid that if they intervene, they may become the bully's next victim. As the following example shows, their fear can be warranted.

Ross

Rick had enjoyed taunting Colby, who was considerably smaller than Rick, for several weeks. One day on the playground, Rick cornered Colby, threatening to beat him up and calling him vile names. Ross walked up and told Rick to knock it off, to leave Colby alone. Rick slowly turned to look at Ross and broke out in a big grin. Rick said, "So, mister wuss here is going to help out the sissy—this is going to be good." Ross said, "Come on, Rick, stop it, everyone knows you are big and can take on everyone else, but that's no reason to pick on Colby. Just leave him alone." Rick replied, "You're right— no sense wasting time on that little creep when I've got a better creep in front of me." At that point, Colby took off into the school. Rick hit Ross hard in the stomach. All the other students on the playground looked away. They were afraid of what might happen if they tried to help Ross.

The second bystander response, guilt, can in some cases be extreme. Seeing another person being hurt or purposefully rejected and doing nothing to help that person can result in remorse and a sense of responsibility. Among the possible long-term reactions are physical symptoms, depression, and avoidance of conflict. Another possible bystander reaction is "learned helplessness," in which bystanders feel unable to have any impact on their own lives or the lives of others. In brief, they give up because they assume whatever they want will be out of their control.

Rachel

Rachel knew that Karen and Hannah were deliberately taunting Keisha, but Rachel didn't know what to do. She was glad she wasn't being tormented by the two of them. Rachel talked to her mother about what was happening and asked what she should do, but her mother told her to keep out of it, it wasn't her business, and besides, they didn't know what Keisha had done to instigate the problem, and it might be Keisha's fault and serve her right for doing whatever she had done. Rachel continued to ignore what was happening to Keisha but felt sad and ashamed for not helping. One day, Keisha stopped coming to school and never returned. Rachel never knew what happened to Keisha, but she also never stopped feeling responsible for having done nothing to help her. Now that Rachel is older, she still feels sad and anxious about not having helped Keisha. Though she has a career as a nurse's assistant and a family of her own, she still has a tendency to shy away from conflict. At work she often gets stuck with holiday shifts because she has never fully developed the ability to stick up for herself.

Empowering Bystanders

Bystanders often know a lot more about the extent, amount, and types of bullying going on in schools than teachers and administrators do, and in our work with schools, we emphasize the importance of addressing bystanders as probably the most important component of a bullying prevention and reduction program.

In neighborhoods, there are never enough police to protect every home and every citizen, but by developing neighborhood watch programs in which community members look out for one another and developing a code of treating people with respect and dignity, we don't need to have police at every house. Similarly, if students are taught to treat one another with respect and dignity and to help take care of those who need help, we don't have to have teachers or other adults looking over the shoulders of children all the time. Of course, it is necessary to act immediately to stop those who engage in bullying behavior—and it is essential to provide support for and protect the targets of bullying. However, if students are taught to treat one another with respect and dignity and to help take care of those who need help, there will be less need for teachers and administrators to supervise.

With encouragement and support, bystanders can be empowered to respond to bullying situations in an effective way. The best way for bystanders to intervene is indirectly—by letting adults know when bullying is taking place, including children who are frequent targets in their play and other activities, and expressing their disapproval of bullying when it is appropriate and safe to do so. It is important to stress that *bystanders should not intervene directly in bullying situations.* Their fears that they may be hurt if they become involved in the situation are often justified.

In one elementary school, we witnessed a positive resolution to a potentially damaging situation. The students were on the playground during recess. Near the monkey bars, two students started to taunt another student from a lower grade. Some of the students who were playing nearby saw this. They felt bad for the younger student, so they decided to tell a teacher. When they told the teacher, the teacher praised them for being concerned about the welfare of their fellow student and quickly put a stop to the bullying.

ACTIVITY 7.5

Initiate a conversation with your child about bullying and aggression in the school. Ask your child to identify those who bully regularly and to tell you where and when bullying tends to take place. Then talk about what it is like to be a bystander in these situations:

▶ Let your child know that it is difficult to witness acts of bullying, even when you aren't the target yourself. Explore the feelings your child has as a bystander.

▶ Discuss things your child can do to help—for example, enlisting the support of a caring adult in the area (a teacher, playground supervisor, or counselor), talking with other bystanders about their experiences, and supporting the child who is targeted once the bullying situation is over.

▶ Be sure to stress that your child should not get involved directly in a bullying situation if there is a chance he or she could be hurt.

Contact the school if your child is reporting a significant problem with bullying, either as a bystander or direct target. Concerned school officials will appreciate this information. If you find that this isn't the case, call the school district.

Follow up on your child's experiences as a bystander and be sure to provide lots of support.

SUMMARY AND CONCLUSIONS

In this chapter, we listed some warning signs for targets and described some things parents of targets can do to help their children. Children who are targeted need immediate protection from their tormentors; they can also benefit from learning skills to avoid and respond effectively to bullying. Assertive communication, including I-messages, and the skill of asking for help are especially important. Targets often lack friends and supporters, and teaching friendship-making skills and strengthening existing friendships are also valuable. Bystanders often feel afraid or guilty. With adult support, they can be empowered to report bullying and help children who are directly targeted cope with their situation.

CHAPTER
8
Parents and Schools

If your child is involved in a bullying situation—as bully, target, or bystander, the problem is most likely taking place at school or on the way to or from school. Especially because we pass laws requiring young people to be in school until a certain age, it is the responsibility of schools to maintain a safe and comfortable learning environment for students. Part of that responsibility is to prevent bullying and intervene rapidly when bullying takes place. This chapter looks at the characteristics of schools that help reduce bullying and other forms of aggression, describes responses schools commonly make to address bullying and the importance of clear rules and consequences, and makes specific suggestions about communicating effectively with your child's school. Finally, it offers suggestions for empowering parents to work together to address the problem of bullying.

Before moving on to those topics, we first should acknowledge the fact that teachers and school administrators have an enormous influence over your child's circumstances, and enlisting the school's assistance to face bullying problems, seek solutions, and work cooperatively can yield excellent results. Although there are exceptions, our overwhelming experience is that teachers and other school personnel really do care greatly about the health, welfare, and learning experiences of their students—and they strive to provide the best classrooms possible.

THE IMPORTANCE OF SCHOOL CLIMATE

Environments, like people, have "personalities" that deeply affect the individuals within them for better or for worse. The school environment, often referred to as the *school climate,* is a product of the interactions among all the members of the school community—administration, teachers and other staff, and students—and the physical qualities of the school building and its surroundings. School climate is important because it appears to be directly related to bullying and aggression—the more positive the climate, the less bullying occurs.

Components of a Positive School Climate

In their book *Bullying Prevention*, Orpinas and Horne describe these components of a positive school climate:

► *Excellence in teaching.* When teachers are expert on their subject matter and are well prepared for their classes, better learning and fewer behavior problems result.

► *School values.* Schools value the people who are there and promote a philosophy with the underlying assumptions that all children can learn (and deserve to be taught well), that all people in school are to be treated with respect and dignity, and that there is no room in the school for aggression, violence, or bullying by anyone.

► *Awareness of strengths and problems.* Administrators and teachers take pride in learning about how their school functions, and this includes being open to identifying what can be improved as well as being proud of the accomplishments and successes they experience.

► *Established policies and accountability.* The school has clear rules and guidelines, and everyone is held accountable for following them.

► *Caring and respect.* The school values diversity and supports appreciation for all people in the school. It demonstrates through modeling that teachers and administrators recognize the value of the school to provide learning and growth opportunities for all students.

► *Positive expectations.* Teachers and other school staff expect positive learning to occur and let students know they expect great outcomes. In some ways, this becomes a self-fulfilling prophecy: People who know others expect high levels of performance generally perform at high levels.

► *Support for teachers.* Administrators are able to demonstrate the same kind of respect, support, and care that teachers are expected to demonstrate toward students.

► *Positive physical environment.* Even though all schools cannot be new and have the latest equipment, they can be clean, safe, and inviting.

The school with a positive climate is an inviting place to be. It is a place where learning occurs, all people are treated with respect and dignity, and a sense of safety and security prevails. Teachers also have an invitational approach to their students: While schools have become more focused on academics recently, teachers still need to be caring people who know and understand their students. When teachers encourage their students to be open and comfortable, they are more likely to share concerns and issues, including worries about being bullied or harassed.

In this type of school, the administration supports teachers and parents and works closely with them to develop plans for addressing problems of bullying, including being willing to contact parents if there are problems. In addition, the school provides a supportive environment where teachers are provided opportunities to increase their knowledge and skill level for addressing classroom management and bullying problems.

ACTIVITY 8.1

Think about the climate in your child's school, then answer the following questions.

► What are your impressions of the interactions among administrators, teachers and other staff, and students?

_____

_____

► What aspects of the physical environment do you notice?

_____

_____

► Overall, do you feel welcome when you visit? If yes, what about the school makes you feel this way? If no, what do you think could help?

_____

_____

If you have concerns about your child's school climate, consider contacting the principal to begin a dialogue.

SCHOOL RESPONSES TO BULLYING

Many schools have instituted bullying prevention and intervention programs, like the Bully Busters program. If so, part of the program will involve maintaining a positive school climate and keeping the focus on positive interactions among all members of the school community. Schools both with and without bullying prevention and intervention programs commonly respond to bullying and other forms of aggression with the following types of actions.

Disciplinary responses

Disciplinary responses include detentions, in-school suspensions, out-of-school suspensions, and, in extreme cases, expulsion.

Historically, these types of consequences have been handed out to students who bully. Without support from adults and efforts to teach more positive ways of reacting, however, these procedures are unlikely to result in much change.

Social skills training

As mentioned earlier in this book, schools sometimes provide social skills training in areas that children who bully and are bullied need. Such skills relate to friendship making, assertiveness, and anger control, among others. Social skills training usually takes place in small groups of students who have been pulled out of regular classrooms, but sometimes whole classes will also participate.

Individual and group counseling

School counselors or school psychologists sometimes provide help to individual students or to small groups of students who share similar issues. Such interventions may focus on various topics, including self-esteem, communication skills, and conflict resolution. If students appear to have severe problems, the counselor or psychologist may suggest a referral to a professional mental health practitioner in the community.

Peer mediation

Peer mediation programs are becoming increasingly popular in schools. In these programs, students are trained in the principles of mediation and, under the supervision of an adult sponsor, help other students resolve their conflicts peacefully. Often peer mediation is part of a school's overall effort to create a safe and supportive educational environment.

CLEAR RULES AND FAIR CONSEQUENCES

Clear rules and fair consequences contribute to a positive school climate—as well as to safety in schools. Following are some examples of clear rules:

► Raise your hand before you speak during a classroom lesson.
► Come to class on time.
► Listen quietly while others are speaking.
► Be quiet in lines, hallways, and rest rooms.
► Call people by their proper names.

Students often complain about rules being "unfair," and sometimes they are. One way to make certain rules are fair is to include students in their development and enforcement. When students are involved with rule making, they are much more likely to endorse and follow rules as they relate to bullying and other behaviors. The same is true for consequences: An excellent way to develop consequences is to have students participate in the process so that they help devise the outcomes. The focus of consequences should be on problem solving ("How can we do this better in the future?") rather than on punishment, for punishment often creates hostility and the belief in those who are punished that the people with the most power always get to have their way. This belief reinforces the notion that coercion and power are the solutions to conflict.

At the classroom level, schools also employ many of the same consequences that you likely also use regularly at home:

- *Time-out:* The student is isolated, such as in a corner of the room or in another room, for a brief period of time. The goal of time-out is not to punish but to interrupt the misbehavior and give the student an opportunity to think about what was done wrong and how it can be done better next time.

- *Removing privileges:* Privileges that may be lost include recess time, free activity time, or time working with other students.

- *Natural consequences:* A natural consequence is a result that occurs naturally—the child who refuses to put on a jacket to go outside in chilly weather will become cold. The child who forgets to register for lunch will miss lunch that day.

- *Logical consequences:* These are consequences that are related to the misbehavior. For example, a student who teases others may be required to apologize for the teasing and then spend some time writing a paper describing the importance of developing friendships and being nice to others.

Just as children expect parents to be fair and to set limits, so do students, and they become irritated when they believe there is inconsistency or unfair delivery of consequences. Teachers and other school staff must take responsibility for consistently and fairly applying rules and consequences. A caveat here, however: We endorse the policy of "zero bullying/zero aggression" in schools, but we do not endorse policies that leave no option for school staff to use their professional judgment in determining consequences for students' misbehavior. We have seen schools in which children have been expelled for bringing prescription drugs to school, thus violating a "no drugs" rule. We have also seen students expelled because they were ganged up on by bullies and fought back. Even though these students were the targets, officially, they violated the "no fighting" rule.

Discuss the rules at school with your child. As you do so, relate the need for rules at school with the need for rules at home. You can ask the following questions:

▶ What are the most important rules in your school? In your classroom?

_____

_____

▶ Which rules seem to be working? Which ones don't?

_____

_____

▶ Are the rules fair? Why or why not?

_____

_____

▶ Do you think the school needs to have new rules? If so, what would they be?

_____

_____

Your child may bring up concerns about the school's rules worth investigating. If so, contact your child's teacher or principal to begin a dialogue.

WHEN A BULLYING SITUATION OCCURS

Parents often report to us that communicating with teachers and other school personnel about a bullying situation at school is very stressful. It's difficult to hear that your child is involved in a bullying situation—whether as target or bully.

If Your Child Is Being Targeted

Parents who learn that their child has been the target of bullying will either hear about it directly, from their child, or from a representative of the school, as in the following example.

Steve

Steve told his parents that he was the target of bullying by two other boys in his third-grade class. The two had been teasing Steve about his heavy stature and his poor athletic ability, and they had called him names in front of other children. At first, his parents were reluctant to contact the school because not only did they believe that school administrators were too busy to have the time or energy to help, they also felt that if they rocked the boat it would cause more problems. However, after talking about it, they decided that it would be best to intervene and help Steve right away instead of waiting until the situation got worse. They contacted the school and were quickly connected with the school counselor who, following a brief phone conversation, invited them in for a more formal meeting with Steve's teacher to gather as much information about the situation as possible. After meeting with the school counselor and Steve's teacher, Steve's parents felt that their concerns had been heard. They were impressed with the fact that a follow-up meeting had been scheduled so quickly.

When a child is the target of bullying, what parents want most is for their child to be protected from further harm—immediately! In Steve's case, the meeting resulted in plans to stop the bullying. Things may not always go so smoothly, however, as the following example illustrates.

Marty

Marty came home from school with a torn shirt and was quiet, withdrawn, and somber. This was the third time in a week that he had not been his usual self. Marilyn, his mom, asked what was going on, and he replied, "Nothing" and said he tore his shirt at recess. She pushed harder for an answer this time. When Marty told her that three boys at school had been harassing him, calling him names, and today started beating on him, she became furious. She picked up the phone and called the school. When she got the principal on the phone, Marilyn began by angrily demanding that the other boys be punished, saying the school personnel were incompetent and that she planned to sue the school. The principal refused to talk to Marilyn while she was so agitated and hung up on her. Now Marty feels very embarrassed and wishes he hadn't said a word to his mother.

Admittedly, this situation is extreme. But because the need to protect their child is so strong, it's sometimes hard for parents to be objective when they enter a dialogue with the school. Attacks and defensiveness rarely work to the benefit of a child who is being bullied, however.

Let's look at how Marilyn might have been of more help to Marty by applying the Big Questions, introduced in chapter 3:

1. What is your goal?
2. What are you doing?
3. Is what you are doing helping you achieve your goal?
4. If not, what can you do differently?

What is your goal?

We feel confident that Marilyn's goal is not to embarrass Marty, nor is it to create hostility between her family and the school. It would be good for Marilyn to sit down, think through what her goal is, and reflect on the goal for a few minutes before taking action. If she had done that, we're certain she would say her goal is to be sure that Marty is safe at school and provided with support in managing a bullying problem that is bigger than he can manage at his current skill level.

What are you doing?

Marilyn becomes very angry and frightened when Marty tells her about his experiences. She acts out her anger by yelling at and threatening the principal. Even though Marilyn is trying to solve the problem, the outcomes are not good for anyone involved. What she has done upsets the principal and embarrasses Marty. If Marilyn keeps her goal in focus as she proceeds to talk to the principal, she will likely be able to state what she is doing quite differently: She is asking the school to assist her in taking steps to help Marty find a better level of security in the school.

Is what you are doing helping you achieve your goal?

Clearly, the steps Marilyn actually took did not work for Marty or for anyone else involved in the situation. The principal became angry, Marilyn stayed upset, and Marty's problems did not go away.

What else can you do?

Marilyn needs to take time to establish a plan that will work to meet her goal of helping Marty. There are many steps she could take, including talking with Marty more about the problem to see if there are things that he might attempt to do differently. She might want to include the school, particularly by talking to Marty's teacher and the school principal—not threatening, but expressing her genuine concern. She might also talk to some other parents to see if their children are experiencing similar problems and ask if they have any ideas. Another way she might help is by enlisting other kids to support Marty so that conflicts might be avoided in the future. Identifying community organizations where Marty could safely learn adaptive skills to manage bullying could also be worthwhile.

If Marilyn's actions don't resolve the difficulty, she may want to consider talking with the superintendent of the school district or to members of the board of education. She may also want to meet with other parents to discuss the problem and see about working together as a team to address the problem. In extreme circumstances, she may even consider moving Marty to another school.

If Your Child Is Engaged in Bullying Behavior

If your child is involved in bullying behavior, you aren't likely to hear about it from him or her. Rather, you'll hear it from the parents of the child who is being bullied or from a school representative. It's understandably hard for parents to hear that their child has been bullying other students. When this happens, parents are often initially skeptical of the report. If you hear this message from your child's teacher, try to keep an open mind while you investigate the situation. The best course is to work with school staff to understand what is happening and then work together to establish a plan to stop the problem as quickly and effectively as possible.

Sheree

When he answered the phone, Sheree's dad was surprised to hear that the caller was his daughter Sheree's middle school counselor, Ms. Tripp. Ms. Tripp told him that Sheree had been the focus of some problems at school for several weeks now and that the problems were becoming worse. The main issue was that Sheree was using her influence among a number of the popular girls to exclude several other girls from activities and to keep them from associating with Sheree and her friends. Sheree first had identified one other girl to exclude, and she did so by spreading misinformation—by saying that the other girl had been bad-mouthing Sheree's friends and so shouldn't be part of the group. Sheree then targeted several other girls in this manner. Anytime someone challenged Sheree, they became the next target. A couple of Sheree's friends had come to Ms. Tripp, not sure what to do and worried that they would become among the excluded. When

Ms. Tripp talked to Sheree about what she had heard, Sheree denied she had done anything wrong at first but then said the others were not worthy of hanging out with Sheree and her friends—they deserved to be treated the way they were.

In this case, Ms. Tripp's decision to call Sheree's parents resulted in their working together to develop a plan to help Sheree. Ms. Tripp made a point to stop by Sheree's class to talk about the importance of treating all people in the school with respect and dignity and met again with Sheree to talk about concerns related to the bullying. Sheree's mother and father agreed to talk with Sheree at home and attempt to understand what was happening and why, as well as what might be done to address the problem.

When they talked, Sheree's parents explained that they were concerned to hear that Sheree was being cruel to some of her friends and was using her influence to exclude others from activities. At first, Sheree denied that this was happening, saying that she and her friends just sometimes got tired of the same people and so didn't hang out with them as much as they used to. Sheree's mom said she understood that could happen, but that it would mean still being polite and friendly with the former friends. Since it seemed Sheree was actually being unkind, Sheree's dad pointed out that people don't usually treat former friends in unfriendly ways unless there is something else going on.

Sheree began crying and said that things were so much more difficult now that she was in middle school—she was afraid people wouldn't like her anymore and that she would have no influence among the other girls. She said she had begun being mean to others in order to make sure her friends would still talk to her. She said she felt guilty but also admitted that it felt "sort of good" to know she had the power to determine who stayed in the group. Sheree's parents suggested that Sheree might benefit by talking with Ms. Tripp about the situation to see if she had suggestions on ways Sheree could feel confident, assured, and accepted without excluding people. Sheree followed through, and Ms. Tripp did indeed have a number of ideas. She continued to meet with Sheree every couple of weeks to talk about how the suggestions were working out and what other ideas Sheree might try.

PARENTS HAVE POWER

Our experience is that when parents band together to express their concern about the welfare of their children, schools begin implementing bullying prevention and intervention programs and establishing other plans to make schools a safer environment. Parents have tremendous influence—if they are willing to use it. When we conduct parent groups in schools, we often hear parents say they wish that others cared as much as they do and that it would be easier if they weren't facing the problems alone. Pretty soon the group realizes that the other parents *are* facing these problems and that they *do* care.

One situation illustrating this point involved the father of a high school student who called and asked if we worked with sexual harassment issues. We explained that we usually didn't but asked him to explain what was happening. He said that his daughter came home from school every day crying because, in her school, boys often touched her and other girls inappropriately in the halls as they changed classes. The father had already talked to the counselor and the principal. Both denied there was a problem, saying the daughter was being too sensitive and that adolescents had to learn to manage themselves—some problems were just a part of life.

We met with the principal and the counselor and suggested that while they might not believe there was a problem, we thought there should be a survey of students to learn how much of an issue actually existed. Further, we pointed out that allowing sexual harassment to occur would be a legal violation that could affect the school's funding and that, surely, the school board would be interested to know that parents were aware of a problem not being addressed by the school. The school refused to agree to a survey, but they did agree to convene a meeting with interested parents to discuss the issue.

The school sent an announcement inviting parents to attend a meeting to discuss reports of inappropriate behavior. When the meeting took place, more than 50 parents and their children attended. The principal began the meeting by saying he thought there wasn't a serious problem. Several female students then stood and graphically described how they had been touched in the hallways. The examples they described were clearly inappropriate, but the principal still said he thought they were exaggerating the problem. At that point, a number of the parents became very angry and vocal. Fortunately, a school counselor stepped in and calmed people down by explaining that the allegations were serious, that there seemed to be consistency among the reports, and that they would need to take schoolwide action to address the problem.

At that point, the principal agreed, and the counselor suggested that they develop a committee of parents, students, teachers, and counselors to review the extent of the problem and develop a plan for addressing it. The committee was formed that evening and began meeting the next day. Within a week, the school adopted a new behavior code, and the school counselors began holding discussions in all classrooms to explain the new rules, why they were important, and the consequences of violating them.

The primary focus of the meeting was sexual harassment, but the parents' questioning resulted in the school's giving increased emphasis to the importance of treating all people with respect and dignity and thus had an impact on other types of bullying as well.

We feel it is extremely important to become involved in your school's parent-teacher organization. In our experience, school officials will mobilize to make changes when they are brought up at a meeting by even a small group of concerned parents. At some schools we have worked with, parents have formed committees to prevent and reduce bullying. Composed of parents, teachers, counselors, and administrators, these committees meet every month or so. Though such meetings do take time, they are extremely effective in creating positive change. Also, the children of those who participate see their parents' concern and involvement and view their parents as models for socially minded, goal-directed success.

ACTIVITY 8.3

Join with other concerned parents in your child's school or school district to discuss ways to support the school's efforts to prevent and intervene with bullying—or to gather information to present to school staff about the need for such a program.

▶ Who is in charge of these programs, and what possibilities for parent involvement exist?

_____

_____

_____

▶ What kinds of information about bullying can the school provide for your review?

_____

_____

_____

Continue to develop communication with other parents and with members of the school administration, staff, and teachers to improve school climate and develop effective ways to prevent and reduce bullying.

SUMMARY AND CONCLUSION

We believe it is essential for parents to establish an open and facilitative communication with the school, preferably before any problems develop. Once the school-family connection exists, it is much easier for families to work with the school to address any problems that may develop. A positive school climate is essential in preventing bullying, and schools should develop clear rules and behavioral guidelines, with students participating in rule making and the determination of consequences. Communicating with the school about your child's involvement in a bullying situation can be difficult, but keeping the Big Questions in mind can help. Finally, parents can be tremendously effective when they come together to work with the school in planning ways to prevent bullying and intervene effectively when it does occur.

Reference

Orpinas, P., & Horne, A. M. (2006). *Bullying prevention: Creating a positive school climate and developing social competence.* Washington, DC: American Psychological Association.

Taking Care of Yourself

You board the airplane and take your seat. In a few minutes, a flight attendant comes on the speaker and says something like this:

> On behalf of the captain and crew of this flight, we welcome you aboard. At this time, make sure that your seat belt is fastened securely, tray tables are in their upright and locked positions, and all personal belongings have been stowed. In case of emergency, this aircraft is equipped with floor lighting directed toward exits and oxygen in case there is a loss of cabin pressure. Should they become necessary, oxygen masks will be released. In this event, pull the mask toward you and place the mask over your face. *If you are traveling with children or others who will need assistance, make certain that your own mask is in place first before assisting them . . .*

Airline personnel know that if you don't take care of yourself in an emergency, you will quickly become unable to care for others. The same is true of parenting. If we are unable to care for ourselves, we soon lose the capacity to care for others. This chapter looks at ways to recognize stress and take care of yourself so you can continue to be effective in helping your child deal with bullying situations—as well as with other challenges.

WHAT IS STRESS?

The most commonly accepted definition of stress is that it is a condition or feeling experienced when a person perceives that demands exceed the personal and social resources that the individual is able to mobilize. Stress is not necessarily a bad thing—it is an unavoidable part of life that can cause us to grow and change in positive ways. But when stress is out of control, it can interfere with our functioning and ability to handle tasks of daily living. It can also contribute to health problems such as high blood pressure, ulcers, fatigue, and headaches.

General recommendations for coping with stress may seem obvious, but because acting on these recommendations is easier said than done, it's important to repeat them here:

131

- ► Get enough sleep.
- ► Eat a well-balanced diet.
- ► Exercise on a regular basis.
- ► Take brief rest periods during the day to relax.
- ► Take vacations away from home and work.
- ► Engage in pleasurable or fun activities every day.
- ► Avoid the excessive use of caffeine and alcohol.

In addition to giving these suggestions, this chapter describes some specific things you can do to manage stress: become aware of the sources of stress, practice stress reduction strategies, and ask for help when you need it.

STRESS AWARENESS

Parents in our groups often tell us that they don't even realize that they are stressed until they are ready to erupt. Stress is cumulative, so it is especially important for us to become aware of sources of stress in our lives so we can take action before stress becomes too much to handle. We experience stress on any one of three different levels: physical, cognitive (thinking), and emotional.

Physical

Take a moment to think how your body feels when it becomes stressed. Does your heart start to beat faster? Does your breathing become shallow? Do you feel shaky? These are all physical symptoms of stress.

Cognitive

Consider for a moment the thoughts that run through your mind when you are feeling stressed. Your mind may begin to race with negative messages that maintain or even increase your level of stress (for example, "I can't stand this" or "I'll never be able to keep my child from being bullied").

Emotional

Usually, we experience a number of feelings when we are stressed. Which words are most descriptive of your own feelings: *anxious, angry, frustrated, tired, bored?* Identifying your feelings will help you manage the stress associated with them. Are you frustrated and angry? If so, an exercise program may help you drain off energy in a positive way. Are you feeling exhausted? In this case, making extra time for rest and relaxation can help.

When we discuss stress with parents, we provide a chart that offers them an opportunity to identify stressors, recognize their seriousness, determine the degree to which they have control over these stressors, and make plans to take action, if appropriate. Consider how one parent, Helen, used this chart, shown in Figure 11, to help her identify a source of stress and decide what she could do about it.

Helen

My daughter had a really hard time getting her homework done at night. I tried everything, but I just couldn't seem to get her to sit down to get it done. I got so angry with her! I'd usually end up all red in the face, screaming at the top of my lungs at her, and that never got us anywhere! When I stopped to think about it, I realized that arguing with my daughter about homework was a big stressor for me—about an 8 on a scale of 10. I did have a fair amount of control over the situation, though (about a 9): I knew if I wanted things to change, I'd have to stop yelling at her. I could hold my tongue and try my best to stay calm. I decided that once I was calm, I would talk to her about what she needed to do. She still has a hard time, but we were able to talk about setting a time to sit down to work. I feel much better about myself now that I can talk to her without getting so angry.

ACTIVITY 9.1

Use Figure 12, on page 135, to help you to identify common stressors in your life. (These may or may not be related to parenting.)

► Work across the chart, filling in the columns and determining how serious the stress is and how much control you have over it. For example, if you are feeling stressed because of conflicts with your boss, it's important to remember that you are not very likely to change your boss!

► In the last column, be sure to come up with reasonable strategies for dealing with the stressors you have identified. To continue the work example, you might not be able to change your boss, but you can change the way you react and respond to the situation, and these changes can result in a reduction of stress.

Figure 11　Helen's Stressor

What is the stressor?	How does it affect me?	Seriousness (1–10)	Influence (1–10)	What can I do?
My daughter won't sit down and do her homework without a fuss.	I get furious and yell at her.	8	9	Calm down and talk to my daughter when I'm not mad anymore

RELAXATION

Everyone knows what *relaxation* means. We hear the word in advertisements encouraging us to take vacation getaways or buy certain chairs or beds—even to rely on prescription drugs. We encourage you to take time alone to think about what you find relaxing. What is it about the event or experience that relaxes you? Can you picture it in your mind and allow your body to become relaxed and calm as you think of the event? Can you define differences between relaxing and having fun? Between relaxing and working? Between relaxation and stress?

Solid evidence exists that learning to be calm and relaxed instead of stressed and anxious is not only possible, but also essential for good health. We teach parents in our groups two techniques to encourage relaxation at a very basic level: The *muscle relaxation technique* involves systematically tensing and relaxing different muscle groups. The *breathe and count technique* encourages relaxation through deep breathing.

We have found that children and adolescents enjoy learning and using these relaxation techniques, too. They particularly enjoy learning them as part of a family activity because the skills become something specific to the family—something the family "owns." We encourage you to practice these skills regularly and to make it a point to present, practice, and review use of the skills on a regular basis in your Family Council meetings or during other family time.

Muscle Relaxation

► First, make certain you are wearing comfortable clothes. Sit comfortably and close your eyes. Become aware of your breathing. Notice how you are breathing and gradually begin to slow down the process, breathing in deeper, longer.

► Tighten your hands into fists. Hold them tight for a few seconds and feel the strength in the muscles. Then relax your hands. Feel

Figure 12 My Stressors

What is the stressor?	How does it affect me?	Seriousness (1–10)	Influence (1–10)	What can I do?

how they are different, how the muscles begin to let go and relax. Do this several times, paying close attention to the differences between the tightened fists and the relaxed hands.

► Tighten your biceps. Make your muscles as tight as you comfortably can. Feel the tightness of the muscles, the stress in the body. Hold your biceps tight for a few seconds and then let the muscles relax, fully and gently. Repeat this process several times.

► Continue to monitor your breathing, paying attention to breathing slowly and deeply.

► Raise your shoulders high and hold them tightly for a few seconds. Feel the tightness in the shoulders and then slowly let them come down and relax. Repeat this process several times.

► Move your head side to side, then slowly turn your head left and right, and as you do feel the neck muscles tighten. Be aware of how the muscles feel as they tighten, then how they feel as they become relaxed. Repeat this process several times.

► Wrinkle your nose, scrunch up your cheeks, and make the tightest face you can. Feel the tightness of the muscles, the energy that goes into the process. Slowly relax your face. Experience how the muscles can slowly let go of the tension they had when you had your face scrunched tightly. Repeat this process several times.

► Push your tongue against the roof of your mouth and at the same time clench your teeth. Try not to clamp down too hard. Feel the tension in your mouth, jaw, and face. Then relax your tongue and jaw. Repeat this process several times.

► Tighten your stomach muscles; tighten them as though you thought someone was going to push you in the stomach and you wanted to have all your muscles as tight as possible. Slowly let the stomach muscles go and relax. Feel the tension flow away from your middle. Do this several times to feel the difference between the tight muscles and relaxed muscles.

► Tighten your seat muscles and feel the muscles. Slowly relax them and let your body sink deeper into the chair you are in, relaxing as you let go and just experience sitting there. Repeat this process.

► Tighten the muscles in your legs: Hold your legs up somewhat off the floor and then tighten the muscles and then relax them. Do this several times.

► Rotate your feet at the ankles in a circle. Reverse the circle and go the other direction, then point your toes. Then point your toes up, experiencing the tightening of the foot and ankle muscles. Relax these muscles. Repeat.

- Focus on your body as a whole and identify any areas that still feel tense or tight and then practice tightening and relaxing those areas, as you have done before.

- Continue to focus on your breathing, slowing down and breathing deeply.

- When you feel very relaxed and at ease, slowly open your eyes. Review the process in your mind and identify how much calmer you feel now than before.

- Repeat this procedure as often as you would like, with as much detail to various muscle groups as is necessary to develop a relaxed and comfortable feeling in each part of your body.

This technique can lead to a deep and full relaxation, in which your muscles let go of tension, your breathing slows down, your head becomes clear, and your whole body becomes calm. It may feel awkward to do this at first, but with practice, you can achieve a deep and satisfying level of relaxation.

Some people do this procedure when they feel stressed; others do it daily as a way to calm their bodies and minds on a regular basis. The full process can take half an hour or more, but many people discover that it's possible to go through an abbreviated sequence in a few minutes, allowing them to practice almost anywhere. When it's not possible to go through the complete or abbreviated muscle relaxation process, you can try the following technique.

Breathe and Count

- Close your eyes. Slowly take a deep breath.

- Hold your breath and slowly begin counting to yourself: 1, 2, 3, 4, and so on, until you become uncomfortable holding your breath.

- Then exhale deeply—slowly release your breath as fully as you can.

- Then slowly count to yourself: 1, 2, 3, 4, and so on, until you again become uncomfortable and need to breathe in.

- Count again. Continue this process for a minute or more.

You will find that you are able to hold your breath longer and then exhale and go without breathing longer as you practice. Most people report this to be a very calming experience. A nice thing about the breathe and count process is that you can use the technique without others' being aware you are doing it. We have had parents who have reported using this process while talking to the parents of a bully. It paid off, for they were able to stay calm and focused rather than become angry and confrontational.

Practice these relaxation techniques during a time when you're calm and won't be disturbed. Try to become aware of how you feel before and after using the techniques.

► The next time you anticipate a stressful situation, use one of the relaxation techniques beforehand. Remember: You can use the breathe and count technique while you're actually in the situation.

► Afterwards, ask yourself how you did: Did using a relaxation technique help? Was it easier to stay centered during the situation? To listen to what others had to say? To express your own thoughts and feelings?

Teach these techniques to your children. Encourage them to use the techniques to calm down and manage stress.

ASKING FOR AND ACCEPTING HELP

Now that we have addressed some ways you can take care of yourself, it is important to consider the importance of having support outside of your family. Parenting isn't easy, and it can become even more challenging when your child is exhibiting bullying behaviors or is the target of bullying.

As a parent, you are in the best position to help your child. However, if you have tried to make changes on your own or as a family and have not been successful, don't give up! If your child is part of the bully-target cycle, this is too important an issue to let go. As with so many things in life that need fixing, this problem doesn't get better with time, just worse. It is wise to continue seeking help if you are not satisfied with the progress you and your family have made on your own.

Sometimes parents have resources available but don't use them because they are afraid of asking for help. They may have been rejected or had negative experiences in the past that keep them from making the contact.

Wanda and Chance

Wanda was having problems with her son, Chance. He was a very active and often aggressive young man who had been troublesome most of his nine years, and he caused problems at home, school, and in the neighborhood. Wanda's husband had mostly ignored the problems because, as he said, "I was just like that when I was young, and I turned out fine." Besides, the dad was big, and because Chance avoided conflict with him, he didn't see many of the same problems Chance's mother did.

Wanda turned to her church for help. The minister explained that the problems were normal childhood issues and that Chance would likely outgrow the problem as he got older. The minister also suggested that the family should spend more time together. While the words were reassuring, they were not particularly helpful. Wanda still had no idea of what to do differently.

One day, Wanda was contacted by Chance's school counselor, who explained that Chance seemed to be bullying other children at school. When Wanda said she could believe it but didn't know what to do, the counselor invited Wanda in to talk about the problem. When they met, Wanda expressed her confusion about what to do with Chance to get him to behave at home, let alone at school. The counselor spent considerable time talking with Wanda about some important issues she could consider:

- ▶ Establishing clear and easily understood rules, guidelines, and expectations for the home

- ▶ Using natural and logical consequences—when Chance misbehaved, being certain there would be immediate consequences to the misbehavior

- ▶ Using time-out, removal of privileges, additional chores, and restrictions on desirable events

- ▶ Establishing a positive reinforcement system for appropriate behavior, along with spending positive time together in reading, games, and sports

The counselor agreed to meet with Wanda weekly for several weeks to monitor how well Wanda was doing in reaching her goals. Although she could become highly discouraged, the support from the counselor helped her stick with her plan. The counselor also talked with Wanda about ways to include her husband in the change plan as well.

ACTIVITY 9.3

In chapter 2, we looked at factors associated with bullying and discussed the importance of understanding your *sphere of influence*—that is, what you can influence and what you can't.

- ▶ Return now to Figure 8, "Helpful Resources," on page 33.

- ► Think again about the potential resources in your school, neighborhood, and community and determine whether you can expand upon them, identifying additional organizations and people who can help.

- ► Add the additional resources you identify to the chart.

Sometimes asking for help is difficult, but if you do need assistance, please don't hesitate to contact these resources.

SUMMARY AND CONCLUSIONS

In this chapter, we talked about how important managing stress is to parents' ability to help their children. Specifically, we defined stress, offered suggestions for becoming aware of stressors and figuring out how to respond to them, described two specific relaxation techniques, and stressed the importance of asking for and accepting help when it's needed. Ultimately, being well and parenting well go hand in hand.

Suggested Resources

Books

Botvin, G. J., Mahalic, S. F., & Grotpeter, J. K. (1998). *Life skills training* (Book 5, Blueprints for Violence Prevention). Center for the Study and Prevention of Violence, Institute of Behavioral Science, University of Colorado at Boulder.

> *This book is helpful in reviewing what programs are effective for developing life skills.*

Christophersen, E. R., & Mortweet, S. L. (2003). *Parenting that works: Building skills that last a lifetime.* Washington, DC: American Psychological Association.

> *For parents and professionals, this book identifies effective methods for reducing behavior problems.*

Cole, J. *Bully trouble.* New York: Random House.

Curwin, R. L., & Mendler, A. N. (1997). *As tough as necessary: Countering violence, aggression, and hostility in our schools.* Alexandria, VA: Association for Supervision and Curriculum Development.

Curwin, R. L., & Mendler, A. N. (1999). *Discipline with dignity.* Alexandria, VA: Association for Supervision and Curriculum Development.

> *The preceding two books were developed to help teachers learn more effective ways of managing discipline in schools. Many of the suggestions provided will work well in the family setting.*

Davis, S. (2007). *Empowering bystanders in bullying prevention.* Champaign, IL: Research Press.

Davis, S. (2007). *Schools where everyone belongs: Practical strategies for reducing bullying* (2nd ed.). Champaign, IL: Research Press.

> *Davis's books offer excellent guidance for creating a positive school climate and for taking steps to involve bystanders to reduce the overall problem of bullying.*

Elias, M., Tobias, S., & Friedlander, B. (1999). *Emotionally intelligent parenting: How to raise a self-disciplined, responsible, socially skilled child.* New York: Three Rivers Press.

Espelage, D. L., & Swearer, S. M. (2004). *Bullying in American schools: A social-ecological perspective on prevention and intervention.* Mahwah, NJ: Erlbaum.

> *This is a very thorough review of programs that have been implemented for bullying reduction in schools.*

Faber, A., & Mazlish, E. (1995). *How to talk so kids can learn at home and at school.* New York: Fireside.

> *A book for parents and teachers on effective adult-child communication.*

Forehand, R., & Long, N. (2002). *Parenting the strong-willed child: The clinically proven five-week program for parents of two- to six-year-olds* (2nd ed.). Chicago: Contemporary Books.

> *An excellent book for parents to help them learn to manage the strong-willed child (and bullies are often strong-willed children).*

Garrity, C., Baris, M., & Porter, W. (2000). *Bully-proofing your child: A parent's guide.* Longmont, CO: Sopris West.

Goldstein, A. P., Glick, B., & Gibbs, J. C. (1998). *Aggression Replacement Training: A comprehensive intervention for aggressive youth.* Champaign, IL: Research Press.

> *This book and the Skillstreaming volumes by Goldstein and associates, listed next, were developed to help teachers and institutional staff teach social skills to children and adolescents, especially skills for reducing anger and aggression. The information provided may be implemented at home as well.*

McGinnis, E., & Goldstein, A. P. (1997). *Skillstreaming the elementary school child: New strategies and perspectives for teaching social skills.* Champaign, IL: Research Press.

Goldstein, A. P., & McGinnis, E. (1997). *Skillstreaming the adolescent: New strategies and perspectives for teaching social skills.* Champaign, IL: Research Press.

Goleman, D. (1995). *Emotional intelligence: Why it can matter more than IQ.* New York: Bantam Books.

> *The publication that popularized the concept of emotional intelligence, this book presents information about how to raise an emotionally intelligent child.*

Greenberg, M. T., Kusche, C. A., & Mihalic, S. (1998). *Promoting alternative thinking strategies (PATHS)* (Book 10, Blueprints for Violence Prevention). Center for the Study and Prevention of Violence, Institute of Behavioral Science, University of Colorado at Boulder.

> *A useful review of programs that have been effective in helping students develop alternative methods of thinking about problem solving.*

Hazler, R. J. (1996). *Breaking the cycle of violence: Interventions for bullying and victimization*. Washington, DC: Accelerated Development.

> *This book was prepared to help teachers and families become more familiar with the problem of bullying and effective means of intervening to stop it.*

Hoover, J., & Oliver, R. (1997). *Bullying prevention handbook: A guide for principals, teachers, and counselors*. Bloomington, IN: National Education Service.

> *Developed for educators, the material provides very useful guidelines for helping address bullying problems and supporting targets of bullying.*

Horne, A. M., Bartolomucci, C. L., & Newman-Carlson, D. (2003). *Bully Busters: A teacher's manual for helping bullies, victims, and bystanders—Grades K–5*. Champaign, IL: Research Press.

Newman, D. A., Horne, A. M., & Bartolomucci, C. L. (2000). *Bully Busters: A teacher's manual for helping bullies, victims, and bystanders—Grades 6–8)*. Champaign, IL: Research Press.

> *Manuals for the Bully Busters program, these books were developed to help teachers and other educators facilitate the reduction of violence in elementary and middle schools.*

McCoy, E. (1997). *What to do . . . when kids are mean to your child*. Pleasantville, NY: Reader's Digest.

> *A very entertaining and interesting book with a lot of "how to" strategies for parents to help their children.*

Meyer, A. L., Farrell, A. D., Northup, W., Kung, E. M., & Plybon, L. (2000). *Promoting non-violence in early adolescence: Responding in peaceful and positive ways*. New York: Kluwer Academic/Plenum Press.

> *Developed primarily for educators in middle schools, this plan for responding in peaceful and positive ways has been an excellent model for developing responsible student behavior.*

Olweus, D. (1993). *Bullying at school: What we know and what we can do* (Understanding Children's Worlds). Cornwall, England: Blackwell.

Olweus, D., & Limber, S. (2002). *Bullying prevention program* (Book 9, Blueprints for Violence Prevention). Center for the Study and Prevention of Violence, Institute of Behavioral Science, University of Colorado at Boulder.

> *The preceding items are a book about and research review of the program developed by Dan Olweus in Scandinavia. This bullying intervention model is the most studied and is used in many schools and communities.*

Orpinas, P., & Horne, A. (2006). *Bullying prevention: Creating a positive school climate and developing social competence.* Washington, DC: American Psychological Association.

> *A thorough overview of the problem of bullying in schools and families, this book provides readers with information about models that have been developed to use in schools, families, and community settings.*

Ross, D. M. (2003). *Childhood bullying and teasing: What school personnel, other professionals, and parents can do* (2nd ed.). Alexandria, VA: American Counseling Association.

> *A comprehensive review of counseling approaches for reducing violence and bullying in school.*

Schmidt, J. J. (1997). *Making and keeping friends: Ready-to-use lessons, stories, and activities for building relationships—Grades 4–8.* West Nyack, NY: Center for Applied Research in Education.

> *A helpful book when assisting young people in learning social skills.*

Shure, M. B. (2000). *Raising a thinking child workbook: Teaching young children how to resolve everyday conflicts and get along with others.* Champaign, IL: Research Press.

Shure, M. B. (2001). *I Can Problem Solve (ICPS): An interpersonal cognitive problem-solving program—Kindergarten and primary grades.* Champaign, IL: Research Press.

> *This book was developed for teachers to help them teach students effective problem-solving strategies. (Two other books by Shure, available from Research Press, detail the process for teaching preschool children and children in the intermediate grades.)*

Shure, M. B. (2001) *Raising a thinking preteen: The "I Can Problem Solve" program for eight- to twelve-year-olds.* New York: Owl Books.

> *For parents of young children and preteens, the preceding two books are based on Shure's effective problem-solving model, which teaches children how to think, not what to think.*

Silberman, M. L. (1995). *When your child is difficult: Solve your toughest child-raising problems with a four-step plan that works.* Champaign, IL: Research Press.

> *A guide for parents and others on how to help difficult children learn more effective behavior patterns.*

Slaby, R. G., Wilson-Brewer, R., & Dash, K. (1994). *Aggressors, victims, and bystanders: Thinking and acting to prevent violence.* Newton, MA: Education Development Center.

> *A well-developed and documented approach to reducing violence and aggression among children and adolescents.*

Voors, W. (2000). *The parent's book about bullying: Changing the course of your child's life.* Center City, MN: Hazelden.

> *Designed for parents whose children have been bullied at school or who are bullies, this easy-to-read book provides very useful information.*

Webster-Doyle, T. (1991). *Why is everybody always picking on me? A guide to handling bullies.* Middlebury, VT: Atrium.

> *A valuable guide for young people to learn more adaptive methods for managing bullying.*

Willard, N. E. (2007). *Cyberbullying and cyberthreats: Responding to the challenge of online social aggression, threats, and distress.* Champaign, IL: Research Press.

> *Primarily developed for educators, this book examines the breadth and depth of cyberbullying and describes steps to take to curb the problem.*

Web Resources

Behavior-management techniques for safe schools. American Federation of Teachers.

www.aft.org/pubs-reports/downloads/teachers/BehMgtFinal.pdf

> *This document explores best practices in reducing bullying in schools and provides behavior management techniques for safe schools.*

Bullying is not a fact of life (CMHS SVP–0052). U.S. Department of Health and Human Services, Substance Abuse and Mental Health Administration.

http://mentalhealth.samhsa.gov/publications/allpubs/SVP%2D0052/

> *This report provides information to parents about bullying and describes positive parenting techniques to foster nonaggressive children.*

Delete cyberbullying. National Crime Prevention Council.

www.ncpc.org/newsroom/current-campaigns/cyberbullying/

> *This article for teens discusses the dangers of cyberbullying. The National Crime Prevention Council site (**www.ncpc.org**) also provides excellent information on the extent and types of bullying, as well as steps that can be taken to reduce the problem.*

"Hit him back" doesn't work: How to handle bullying behavior.

www.menningerclinic.com/resources/bullying.htm

> *In addition to this article, the Menninger Clinic includes information on the Peaceful Schools Program, a powerful school and family intervention designed to reduce bullying.*

Web Sites

American Association of University Women

www.aauw.org

> *This Web site provides important information about the effects of bullying and other forms of harassment against girls and young women. Includes two reports on bullying and sexual harassment useful for helping parents and teachers address problems girls have in school.*

American Psychological Association

www.apa.org/topics/topicbully

> *This section of the APA Web site provides parents with recommendations and suggestions for working with their child to reduce the problem of bullying and victimization.*

Annie E. Casey Foundation

www.aecf.org

> *Kids Count, a project of the foundation, provides policymakers and citizens with benchmarks of child well-being in order to enrich local, state, and national discussions concerning ways to secure better futures for all children. For the project description, search **www.aecf.org/MajorInitiatives/KIDSCOUNT.aspx**.*

Bullying in Schools

www.education.unisa.edu.au/bullying

> *Australian researchers and educators have been addressing the problem of bullying for a long time. This link from the University of South Australia site includes excellent information about bullying and lists Dr. Ken Rigby's materials for teachers and parents.*

Bully Online

www.bullyonline.org

> *This Web site provides information about such bullying-related issues as school bullying, child bullying, and bullycide.*

California Department of Education

www.cde.ca.gov

> *This site includes a section on training, resources, and technical assistance in the establishment of a school/community environment that is physically and emotionally safe and conducive to learning. Go to **www.cde.ca.gov/ls/ss/se/** for relevant information.*

Center for Effective Collaboration and Practice

http://cecp.air.org

> *The mission of this organization is to support and promote a reoriented national preparedness to foster the development and the adjustment of children with or at risk of developing serious emotional disturbance. For school violence and prevention information, go to* **http://ccep.air.org/school_violence.asp**.

Center for Safe and Responsible Internet Use

www.cyberbully.org

> *Defines cyberbullying and provides resources for educators, parents, and children to combat Internet bullying. The site also provides links to media coverage of Internet bullying.*

Committee for Children

www.cfchildren.org/issues/bully

> *Includes materials specifically developed to assist parents with bullying problems and offers resource papers describing parenting tips and ways to help children deal with bullying. For the pages on bullying, go to* **www.cfchildren.org/issues/bully**.

Hamilton Fish Institute

www.hamfish.org

> *Administered by the School of Education and Human Development at George Washington University and funded by the U.S. Department of Justice, this site is a resource for research on and development of school violence prevention strategies.*

Hoover's Bully Blog

www.hoovbully.blogspot.com

> *This blog provides information on bullying resources, workshops and training, and other materials for helping families and teachers reduce bullying.*

Internet Super Heroes

www.internetsuperheroes.com

> *Informative and entertaining, this site uses comic-type cartoon heroes to teach children about Internet safety.*

I-Safe America

www.isafe.org

> *Provides Internet safety information to kids and teens, educators and parents. It also includes a chat room for teens and links to other related sites.*

KidsHealth

www.kidshealth.com

> *Developed to provide medical and health-related information for parents, this site offers helpful materials on bullying, including parent guides that pinpoint the type of bullying that occurs at different ages. Try this Web page: www.kidshealth.org/kid/feeling/emotion/bullies.html.*

McGruff's Blog

www.mcgruff.org

> *This blog, sponsored by the National Crime Prevention Center, uses cartoons and games to educate children about bullying and aggression. It offers advice on how to deal with bullies and has an online comic book about how to use different techniques.*

Minnesota Center against Violence and Abuse

www.mincava.umn.edu

> *This clearinghouse provides an extensive pool of up-to-date educational resources about all types of violence. It includes higher education syllabi, published research, funding sources, upcoming training events, individuals or organizations serving as resources, and searchable databases with over a thousand training manuals, videos, and other educational materials.*

National Center for Victims of Crime

www.ncvc.org

> *The NCVC is the nation's leading resource and advocacy organization for crime victims. Described on this site, the Teen Victim Project provides information to help victim assistance providers, law enforcement personnel, and other professionals provide informed, culturally competent, and developmentally appropriate responses to teen victims and their families.*

National Crime Justice Reference Service

www.ncjrs.gov

> *This site is a federally funded resource offering justice and substance abuse information to support research, policy, and program development worldwide. Several bullying-related articles are abstracted or available as full-text publications.*

National Education Association

www.nea.org/schoolsafety

> *The school safety section of this Web site is a clearinghouse for information on the topic of school safety. Among the topics*

addressed are safe environments, emergency preparedness, community coalitions, and positive school-community relations.

National Parent-Teacher Association

www.pta.org

This site provides specific information about bullying and provides resources to more than six million PTA members, including parents, students, educators, and citizens who are active in schools and communities.

National Youth Violence Prevention Resource Center

www.safeyouth.org

This very informative site has information about useful intervention strategies and lists additional sites that provide extensive information about the problem.

Stop Bullying Now

www.stopbullyingnow.hrsa.gov

This site describes a number of bullying reduction programs that are available to help schools and families understand and intervene in the problem of bullying.

Target Bullying

www.targetbully.com

Developed by Dr. Susan Swearer, this site describes a bullying prevention and intervention program developed to reduce the bullying problem in schools. It provides valuable resources and contact information for implementing a bullying prevention program.

WiredKids

www.wiredkids.org

This site is designed to help children and others learn safe Internet use and how to protect themselves against Internet abuse.

WiredSafety

www.wiredsafety.org

This site provides information on cybersafety and cyberstalking and provides information about establishing online safety procedures.

About the Authors

Arthur (Andy) M. Horne received his Ph.D. from Southern Illinois University in 1971. He taught at Indiana State University from 1971–1989, where he served as a member of the faculty and director of training of the counseling psychology program, as well as a member of the marriage and family therapy training program. In 1989, Andy joined the faculty of the University of Georgia, serving as department head and director of training for the counseling psychology program and as a coordinator of the marriage and family therapy certificate program. He is the former president of the Association for Specialists in Group Work and the Division of Group Psychology and Group Psychotherapy of the American Psychological Association. Coauthor of nine books and coeditor of six, he has published more than 100 articles on working with children, families, schools, and community agencies. He has directed several large research programs examining the reduction of aggression and violence in families and schools and has directed the Bully Prevention Program at the University of Georgia for the past decade. Andy enjoys conducting training, supervising, and presenting on bullying prevention approaches. He and his family enjoy travel and storytelling.

Jennifer L. Stoddard earned a bachelor's degree in psychology from Augusta College, a master's degree in experimental psychology from Augusta State University, and a Ph.D. in counseling psychology from the University of Georgia. She completed a predoctoral internship at the Medical College of Georgia and Department of Veterans Affairs Medical Center Clinical Psychology Residency Consortium and a postdoctoral fellowship in clinical health psychology from Walton Rehabilitation Health System. Currently, she is a licensed psychologist working in a medical setting and part-time faculty in the psychology department at Augusta State University. She has worked with the Bully Busters program for six years and is a co-developer of the family bullying prevention program. Her doctoral dissertation evaluated the effectiveness of a multiple-family group intervention for first-time juvenile offenders, which included 94 youth and their families. In 2006, she won the APA Division 17 Prevention Section's Outstanding Research Award for this research. Her professional areas of interest include prevention and reduction of violence and aggression in schools and families, health promotion, and the relationship between mental health and physical illness. When she is not working, Jennifer enjoys spending time with family, kayaking, and cycling.

Christopher D. Bell received a bachelor's degree in psychology from the University of Nebraska–Lincoln and a master's degree in clinical psychology from Millersville University. He is currently completing his doctoral studies in counseling psychology at the University of Georgia and is a predoctoral psychology intern at the Medical College of Georgia and Department of Veterans Affairs Medical Center Clinical Psychology Consortium. Over the past several years, Chris has worked as both a clinician and researcher with children and adolescents who have emotional difficulties that relate to aggression and bullying. He has worked with the Bully Busters program for four years and is a co-developer of the family bullying prevention program. His dissertation, which evaluated the implementation of a bullying and aggression reduction program involving over 60 teachers and 400 students at a middle school, won the 2007 APA Division 17 Prevention Section's Outstanding Research Award. His specific area of professional interest is working with children and their families to reduce aggression and increase psychological wellness. When he is not working as a psychologist, he enjoys films and literature and playing with his dog, Oola.